# FIGURATIVELY SPEAKING

## Thesaurus of
## Expressions & Phrases

Fresh Ink Group's Collection of 7,500+
Figures of Speech, Catchphrases,
Idioms, and Colloquialisms Sorted
by Meaning & Context

# FIGURATIVELY SPEAKING

## Thesaurus of
## Expressions & Phrases

**Fresh Ink Group's Collection of 7,500+
Figures of Speech, Catchphrases,
Idioms, and Colloquialisms Sorted
by Meaning & Context**

**J. Ajlouny**

**Fresh Ink** Group
Guntersville

FIGURATIVELY SPEAKING
**Thesaurus of Expressions & Phrases**

**Fresh Ink Group's Collection of 7,500+ Figures of Speech,
Catchphrases, Idioms, and Colloquialisms
Sorted by Meaning & Context**

Copyright © 2017, 2000
by J. Ajlouny
All rights reserved

Fresh Ink Group
An Imprint of:
The Fresh Ink Group, LLC
Box 931
Guntersville, AL 35976
Email: info@FreshInkGroup.com
FreshInkGroup.com

Edition 1.0     2000
Edition 2.0     2017

Book design by Ann E. Stewart

Cover design by Stephen Geez

BISAC Subject Headings:
REF019000 REFERENCE / Quotations
LAN014000 LANGUAGE ARTS & DISCIPLINES / Reference
REF022000 REFERENCE / Thesauri

Library of Congress Control Number: 2017917109

ISBN: 978-1-947867-06-2 Paper-cover
ISBN: 978-1-396442-71-3 Hard Cover
ISBN: 978-1-396442-72-0 eBook Editions

Dedicated to everyone who has had
to do battle to safeguard a dream.

# Contents

# Summary of Contents

# Preface

There is a story, the truth of which I cannot guarantee, that has the great American novelist Henry James asking for his *Roget's Thesaurus* from his death bed. He was apparently not convinced his doctor's diagnosis was stated accurately. With infirm hands and a heavy heart he supposedly searched for a synonym for the word paralytic. No doubt his career as a writer convinced him of the inestimable value of a thesaurus. Can any writer believe less?

This thesaurus is a bit different than Roget's but I doubt you'll find it any less useful. Peter Mark Roget's genius was that he was the first to see the utility of a reference book that listed words not by their definitions as in a dictionary, but by the context of their use. The object, he wrote in the preface to his seminal 1852 edition, was to "find the word or words (sic. for an idea) by which that idea may be most fitly and aptly expressed." Considering the fact that his work enjoyed 28 editions during his lifetime (1779-1896), it's clear he was on to something. The hundreds of editions, imitations and variations published since then attest to the lasting excellence of his original scheme. As a system of logically ordered categories it is brilliant. And to the delight of millions, it remains both useful and comprehensive.

In preparing this collection of expressions and phrases it was my intention to emulate Roget's scheme, though I chose not to copy his categories. On the following pages you will find a Tutorial which explains how to use this work. It is my fervent hope you'll find it helpful and practical. A reference work such as this should be viewed as a tool. It should be of great use to writers and public speakers. On the other hand, I hope the average citizen will find it useful too. Anybody who wishes to add a touch of the vernacular to their writing or speech will find plenty of suggestions here.

A figure of speech is an expression in which the words are used, not in their literal sense, to create a more forceful or dramatic meaning. They are often in the form of metaphors, similes and hyperbole. Metaphors, as you'll likely recall, are figures of speech in which a word is transferred from the object it ordinarily designates to an object it may designate only by implicit comparison. "A fountain of knowledge," is a good example. "Stretching the truth," is another.

Similes are created when we use words that compare or describe two unlike things with the conjunctive "like" or "as". "She barked like a dog" and "He was as happy as a pig in mud" are examples of simple similes. We use them all day long as figures of speech. Hyperbole is nothing but exaggeration, typically using colorful, over-the-top language. Of course most of the thousands of entries listed herein don't neatly fit any of the above models. They are simply well worn idioms that have found a way into the most common version of the English language. The real chore was not in collecting them. To a logophile like myself, that's the easy part. The chore was to find a system for classifying them so that the book is easy to use. I don't profess to having found the key here. I'm no Roget; the categories are my own and seemed fitting when I came up with them. The fact that I changed them so frequently proves to me the job is probably not done. It'll likely remain undone. I challenge the reader to take up the task and do me better.

For their assistance (and willingness to share the blame) I thank several faithful colleagues: Gwen Foss, my chief assistant; Angela Booterbaugh, her successor; Jim Blunt of ABC Editors for whipping it all into shape; and James Conlon for suggesting the idea in the first place. Without their help and support this book would never have seen the proverbial light of day. You see, the fact that I should use such a phrase in describing the chore this compilation entailed proves my point. Figures of speech are worthy of organizing because they are so widely used. Establishing a system of order that permits one to research them for the purpose of finding one's intended meaning is a cause worth celebrating.

# Introduction

This book would not exist if not for the fact that when people talk we like to use figures of speech. Plain old speech gets boring after a while, so folks like to spice up their conversation a bit by describing people, places and things in figurative, colorful language.

A figure of speech is an expression in which words are used, not in their literal sense, but to create a more forceful or dramatic image, as a metaphor, simile, or hyperbole.

A metaphor is a figure of speech in which a term is transferred from the object it ordinarily designates to an object it may designate only by implicit comparison or analogy.

A simile is a figure of speech in which two essentially unlike things are compared, the comparison being made explicit typically by the use of the introductory 'like' or 'as'.

Hyperbole is an exaggeration or extravagant statement used as a figure of speech.

And of course, a thesaurus is a book of selected words or concepts. In this book, the selection is of figures of speech and illustrative language used in common expressions and phrases.

Here is an example of some of the figures of speech you can expect to see in this thesaurus:

| | |
|---|---|
| Mountains of information | (metaphor) |
| Stubborn as a mule | (simile) |
| Beats a story to death | (hyperbole) |

Whenever you need to find an apt phrase to describe someone or something, consult this book; that is its purpose.

It is the fervent hope of the editor that this collection will find its way on to the crowded bookshelves of writers everywhere. For it is there that the fruits of every solemn researcher's efforts can best be utilized, not for gathering dust, but for quick and handy reference.

# Tutorial

You may be wondering how to go about using this book. There are several different ways you can approach it.

If you have plenty of time, you could read it from front to back just like any other book. If you don't have the time or inclination to read the whole thing straight through, you can scan the contents and find a main topic that interests you, and turn to that section. If you're extremely short on time, you can turn to the rear index and look up a specific topic that catches your eye, and turn to the page number listed.

There are 17 main topic headings divided into 177 specific topic listings.

The main topics are: Attitudes, Body Types, Competition, Creature Comforts, Drinking, Ethics or Lack Thereof, Influence, Life / Health / Death, Mental States, Money, Personal Space, Personality Types, Speech, Thinking, Power, Time, Trouble / Turmoil/Commotion, and The World of Work. To find page numbers for main topics, look on the Contents pages.

Some of the specific topics are: Lean and Lithe People, Perfect People, Fleshed Out People, Agile and Coordinated People, Awkward People, Old Folks, and The Body Beautiful. These all fall under the main topic of Body Types, which is section II.

For a complete list of the specific topic listings, turn to the Summary of Contents page or the topical index for an alphabetical arrangement.

## HOW THE TOPIC PAGES ARE ARRANGED

The specific topic pages have been arranged for ease in reading and researching. Each specific topic is comprised of four sections. The first is the topic header in large capital letters. The second section lists some synonyms underneath a caption. The third section lists characteristics of the topic. The fourth section lists other descriptors. See partial example below.

## A SAD PERSON

### A SAD PERSON IS A:

Constant Complainer, Depressed Person, Down in the Dumps, Gloomy Gus, Kill-Joy, Merchant of Gloom

## AND CAN BE CHARACTERIZED BY THE FOLLOWING:

- Anxiously awaits his doom
- Believes the world owes him a living
- Bemoans his fate
- Sings the blues

## OR CAN BE DESCRIBED AS:

- Complaining
- Depressed
- Down in the dumps
- Malcontented
- Unhappy

The above example is only a partial sample of the specific topic but is enough to give you an idea of how the book is set up. This collection will make you chuckle, especially when you see a figure of speech somewhere which perfectly describes yourself or someone you know! Any time you need just the perfect phrase to describe someone or something, just reach for this book and you're sure to find it.

# I
# ATTITUDES

# ASSIST SOMEONE ON THEIR WAY

**WHEN YOU ASSIST SOMEONE ON THEIR WAY, YOU ARE A:**

Booster, Brother, Buddy, Cheerleader, Facilitator, Friend In Need, Good Samaritan, Helping Hand, Mentor, Promoter, Saint, Sister, Sponsor.

**AND CAN BE CHARACTERIZED BY THE FOLLOWING:**

- Check up on him
- Even the playing field for him
- Give him a boost
- Give him a hand
- Give him a hand up
- Give him a helping hand
- Give him a kind word
- Give him a leg up
- Give him a pat on the back
- Get in his comer
- Go to bat for him
- Grease the wheels for him
- Help him over the hurdles
- Lead the way
- Light the way
- Make the path smoother
- Offer your services
- Open doors for him
- Pave the way for him
- Point him in the right direction
- Point the way
- Promote his cause
- Pump him up
- Put in a good word
- Relax the rules
- Ride shotgun for him
- Run interference for him
- Share his load
- Smooth the way for him
- Speak in his behalf
- Stand behind him
- Stand by his side
- Step in the breach for him
- Stick up for him
- Take his side
- Take up for him
- Teach him the ropes
- Teach him the tricks of the trade
- Use your good offices to help

**OR CAN BE DESCRIBED AS:**

- An advocate
- An angel
- A blessing in disguise

# BE PERSISTENT AND DETERMINED

## WHEN YOU ARE PERSISTENT AND DETERMINED, YOU ARE A:

Bull Dog, Pillar Of Strength, Pit Bull, Rock Of Gibraltar.

## AND CAN BE CHARACTERIZED BY THE FOLLOWING:

- Circle the wagons
- Cling to your position
- Dig your heels in
- Dig in for the long haul
- Don't give ground
- Don't take "no" for an answer
- Draw a line in the sand
- Grit your teeth
- Hang in there
- Hang on like a pit bull
- Hold the fort
- Plant both feet firmly on the ground
- Refuse to back off
- Stand your ground
- Stand pat
- Stand up for what you believe
- Stay in the fight
- Stay the course
- Stick it out
- Stick to your demands
- Stick to your guns
- Take a firm stand
- Take a hard line
- Try and try again
- Wage a constant battle
- Work at it day and night

## OR CAN BE DESCRIBED AS:

- See it through to the end
- Set your jaw
- Immovable
- Unflinching

# MOVE CAUTIOUSLY OR BE ALERT

**WHEN YOU MOVE CAUTIOUSLY OR ARE ALERT, YOU ARE:**

Keeping Your Guard Up, On The Lookout, Watching Your Back, Watching Your Step.

**AND CAN BE CHARACTERIZED BY THE FOLLOWING:**

- Avoid the pitfalls
- Be careful
- Cover your rear
- Don't burn your bridges behind you
- Don't get backed into a comer
- Ease your way along
- Exercise caution
- Feel your way along
- Have eyes in the back of your head
- Keep a weather-eye out
- Keep an ear to the ground
- Keep a finger on the pulse
- Keep a finger on the trigger
- Keep a hand on the hilt
- Keep your ears open
- Keep your ears tuned
- Keep your eyes peeled
- Keep your guard up
- Keep your options open
- Keep your pistol cocked
- Keep your powder dry
- Keep your wits about you
- Look before you leap
- Look over your shoulder
- Make sure the coast is clear
- On the lookout
- Play it close to the vest
- Put a finger in the wind
- Put a toe in the water
- Send up a trial balloon
- Sharpen your senses
- Size up the situation
- Sleep with one eye open
- Stay at the ready
- Stay awake
- Step lightly
- Take nothing for granted
- Taste before you swallow
- Test the waters
- Walk close to the wall
- Walk on eggs
- Walk on tippy-toes
- Walk softly and carry a big stick
- Watch your back
- Watch your step

## OR CAN BE DESCRIBED AS:

- Hesitant
- Leary
- Non-trusting

- Reticent
- Skeptical
- Wary

# BE SUBMISSIVE TO SOMEONE

## WHEN YOU ARE BEING SUBMISSIVE TO SOMEONE, YOU AREA:

Beggar, Boot-Licker, Brown-Nose, Fall Guy, Foot Kisser, Lackey, Lamb, Mouse, Patsy, Plaything, Slave, Timid Soul, Whipping Boy, Wimp.

## AND CAN BE CHARACTERIZED BY THE FOLLOWING:

- Act like a robot
- Be a mouse instead of a man
- Be a slave to his desires
- Be afraid to open your mouth
- Be at his beck and call
- Be constantly under his thumb
- Be pushed in the background
  Be teacher's pet
- Bend over backwards to please him
- Bow and scrape before him
- Butter him up
- Carry his bags
- Cater to his every wish
- Come hat-in-hand
- Come to him on bended knee
- Cozy up to him
- Crawl to him
- Curry favor with him
- Doff your cap to him

- Eat dirt for him
- Eat humble pie for him
- Give up your self respect
- Go out of your way to please him
- Grovel before him
- Handle him with kid gloves
- Hang around him
- Hang on his every word
- Have his foot on your neck
- Have no mind of your own
- His wish is your command
- Humble yourself before him
- Jump when he snaps his fingers
- Kiss his ass
- Kiss his feet
- Kneel before him
- Kow-tow to him
- Lay out the red carpet for him

- Let him brow-beat you
- Let him buffalo you
- Let him bully you
- Let him push you around
- Let him put you down
- Let him run rough-shod over you
- Let him step on you
- Let him walk all over you
- Lick his boots
- Live under the lash
- Look up to him
- Never question his acts
- Place him on a pedestal
- Play up to him
- Play second fiddle to him
- Polish the apple
- Praise him to the sky
- Put up with his shenanigans
- Sacrifice yourself lfor his wants
- Shine his shoes
- Shine up to him
- Shrivel to his presence
- Stay under his thumb
- Step aside for him
- Submit to his whims
- Suck up to him
- Suffer his indignities
- Suffer in silence
- Surrender your pride
- Swallow your pride
- Take a back seat to him
- Take his guff
- Think he can do no wrong
- Tolerate his insults
- Treat him like a little tin god
- Treat him like royalty
- Wait on him hand and glove

**OR CAN BE DESCRIBED AS:**

- An apple polisher
- An errand-boy
- Second fiddle

# MAKE A COMEBACK

**WHEN YOU MAKE A COMEBACK, YOU:**

Arise From The Ashes, Get A Fresh Start, Get Back On Your Horse, Pick Up The Pieces, Put The Past Behind You, Try Again.

**AND CAN BE CHARACTERIZED BY THE FOLLOWING:**

- Come up smelling roses
- Believe every knock is a boost
- Get it back on track
- Get it out of your system

- Know it's an ill wind blows no good
- Learned from experience
- No sense beating a dead horse
- No sense crying over spilled milk
- Put the past behind you
- Put your nose to the grindstone
- Put your shoulder to the wheel

- That's the way the ball bounces
- That's the way the cookie crumbles
- Try and try again
- Used some elbow grease
- Used some street smarts
- Used the tricks of the trade
- Will get it right this time

**OR CAN BE DESCRIBED AS:**

- A comeback kid
- A go getter
- Older and wiser

# MINDFUL OF YOUR NEEDS

**WHEN YOU'RE MINDFUL OF YOUR OWN NEEDS, YOU:**

Do What's Best For You, Fare For Yourself, Look Out For Number One, Take A Back Seat To No One.

**AND CAN BE CHARACTERIZED BY THE FOLLOWING:**

- Call your own shots
- Chart your own course
- Cut the apron strings
- Decide for yourself
- Depend on yourself
- Do a solo act
- Do it your way
- Do what you see fit
- Figure it out for yourself
- Follow your instincts
- Lean on no one
- Listen to your conscience
- Make it on your own

- Make up your own mind
- Make your own bed and lie in it
- Make your own way
- Make your presence known
- Mind your own affairs
- Muddle through by yourself
- Paddle your own canoe
- Play second fiddle to no one
- Play your own hand
- Pull your own weight
- Pull yourself up by your bootstraps

- Put yourself first
- Rely on your own counsel
- Set your own agenda
- Stand on your own two feet
- Stand up for your rights

- Strike out on your own
- Throw away your crutch
- Tie your own shoes
- Write your own ticket

## OR CAN BE DESCRIBED AS:

- Independent
- Proud

- Self serving Self aware
- Self serving

# UNMINDFUL OF OTHERS

## WHEN YOU ARE UNMINDFUL OF OTHERS, YOU:

Do Unto Others Before They Do Unto You, Get A Leg Up On Someone, Go For The Jugular, Look Out For Number One.

## AND CAN BE CHARACTERIZED BY THE FOLLOWING:

- All's fair in love and war
- Believe a good loser is a loser
- Believe God helps those who help themselves
- Get it while the getting is good
- Get there firstest with the mostest
- Every man for himself
- I've got my own problems
- Kill or be killed
- Let him shift for himself
- Let the devil take the hindmost
- Might makes right

- Never give a sucker an even break
- Nice guys finish last
- Nice guys never win
- No skin off my nose
- Shoot first and ask questions later
- Stick it to him
- That's your problem
- To the victor belong the spoils
- What he doesn't know won't hurt
- Him
- What's in it for me?

## OR CAN BE DESCRIBED AS:

- A climber
- Neglectful

- Not your brother's keeper selfish

# POSITIVE NEGATIVES

## WHEN YOU USE POSITIVE NEGATIVES, YOU:

Exaggerate, Use Sarcasm.

## AND CAN BE CHARACTERIZED BY THE FOLLOWING:

- Absolutely not!
- Don't even think it
- Get it out of your mind
- No not never
- No way—no how
- Not a Chinaman's chance
- Not a snowball's chance in hell
- Not by a long shot
- Not by the wildest flight of your imagination
- Not even close
- Not even if I could
- Not even in your dreams
- Not for all the money in the world
- Not for all the tea in China
- Not if he were the last man onearth
- Not of my life depended on it

- Not if you value your life
- Not for love or money
- Not in a million years
- Not in your lifetime
- Not in your wildest dreams
- Not now or ever
- Not on this planet
- Not on your life
- Not while I have anything to say about it
- Not while I'm alive.
- Not while there's a breath of life in me.
- You can't be serious
- You don't have a prayer
- You have got to be kidding
- You're jesting—I'm sure.
- You're out of your mind
- You're out of your tree!

## OR CAN BE DESCRIBED AS:

- Being absurd

# TO NEGATE

## WHEN YOU NEGATE SOMETHING, YOU:

Cancel It, Give It Thumbs Down, Nix It, Oppose It, Rule It Out, Shoot It Down, Veto It.

## AND CAN BE CHARACTERIZED BY THE FOLLOWING:

- Bad mouth it
- Blast it
- Blow it away
- Blow it out of the water
- Boo it
- Boot it out
- Bomb it
- Bury it
- Cancel it
- Cut it off
- Deny it
- File it in the circular file
- Flush it down the tube
- Give it short shrift
- Give it the axe
- Give it the kiss of death
- Ignore it
- Junk it
- Kick it out
- Kill it
- Laugh it out
- Pick it to pieces
- Pooh-pooh it
- Pull the plug on it
- Refuse it outright
- Reject it out of hand
- Scrap it
- Scratch it
- Scuttle it
- Shoot it full of holes
- Shut it down
- Sink it
- Skunk it
- Slough it off
- Submarine it
- Tear it to shreds
- Throw it on the scrap heap
- Toss it out
- Trash it
- Turn it down

## OR CAN BE DESCRIBED AS:

- Giving it the boot

# TO DISLIKE

## WHEN YOU DISLIKE SOMETHING:

It Leaves You Cold, It's Not Your Cup Of Tea, It's Not Your Style, It Turns You Off.

## AND CAN BE CHARACTERIZEDBY THE FOLLOWING:

- Disgusting
- Disturbs me
- Doesn't cut it
- Doesn't excite me
- Doesn't suit me
- Doesn't turn me on
- Get it out of my sight
- Gives me goose pimples
- I find it distasteful
- I wouldn't lose any sleep over it
- It has a long way to go
- It's a bummer
- It's only so-so
- It's the pits
- I've seen better
- Leaves a bad taste in my mouth
- Leaves a lot to be desired
- Makes me want to heave
- Makes my blood run cold
- Makes my skin crawl
- Neither here nor there
- Not earth-shaking
- Not so hot
- Nothing exceptional
- Nothing to write home about
- Plain old garden variety
- Pretty run of the mill
- Revolting
- Scroungy
- Won't win any blue ribbons
- Wouldn't dirty my hands on it
- Wouldn't go out of my way for it
- Wouldn't touch it with a ten-foot pole

## OR CAN BE DESCRIBED AS:

- An aversion

# IGNORE A WRONGDOING

## WHEN YOU IGNORE A WRONGDOING, YOU:

Bury Your Head In The Sand, Look The Other Way, Pretend Not To Notice, Put Blinders On.

## AND CAN BE CHARACTERIZED BY THE FOLLOWING:

- Can't get involved
- Can't lose any sleep over it
- Can't let it bother me
- Couldn't care less
- Didn't hear a thing
- Didn't see a thing
- Don't know anything
- I have enough troubles of my own!
- My knowing makes no difference
- No skin off my nose
- None of my business
- Not my concern
- Not my problem
- Nothing I can do about it
- Overlook it
- See no evil, hear no evil, speak no evil
- Shut it out of your mind
- That's notta my job
- Tune out
- Wear rose-colored glasses
- What can I do about it anyway?
- What they don't know won't hurt them

## OR CAN BE DESCRIBED AS:

- Refusing to see what's there

# HUMBLE YOURSELF

## WHEN YOU HUMBLE YOURSELF, YOU:

Admit Your Shortcomings, Face Yourself in The Mirror, Face Up To Your Faults, Swallow Your Pride.

## AND CAN BE CHARACTERIZED BY THE FOLLOWING:

- Ask for a second chance
- Beg someone's forgiveness
- Clean the slate
- Come down to earth
- Come hat-in-hand
- Come on bended knee
- Come to terms with yourself
- Eat dirt
- Eat humble pie
- Eat your words
- Face the music
- Get off your high horse
- Get on the straight and narrow
- Get real
- Get your act together
- Grovel before someone
- Kick your habits
- Make a new start
- Make amends
- Pull in your horns
- Pull yourself together
- Say your mea culpas
- Shape up
- Straighten yourself out
- Swallow a bitter pill
- Take it like a man
- Take it on the chin
- Take what's coming to you
- Take your lumps
- Take your medicine
- Throw yourself on one's mercy
- Turn over a new leaf
- Wear sack-cloth and ashes

## OR CAN BE DESCRIBED AS:

- Giving yourself a new start
- You're ready to change your tune

# ALL ABOUT LAUGHTER

**WHEN YOU LAUGH, YOU ARE:**

Amused, Chortling, Chuckling, Cracked Up, Giggling, Grinning, Roaring, Rolling In The Aisles, Smiling, Snickering, Tickled, Tittering.

**AND CAN BE CHARACTERIZED BY THE FOLLOWING:**

- Bust up laughing
- Have a belly laugh
- Die laughing
- Double up in laughter
- Fall out of your chair laughing
- Funnier than a barrel of monkeys
- Get a bang out of it
- Get a kick out of it
- Get knocked out of your seatlaughing
- Get sore cheeks from laughing
- Go into convulsions over it
- Have a belly laugh
- Have to hold your sides from laughing
- Howl over it
- Hurts your sides
- Hysterical
- I kicked the slats out of my crib the first time I heard it
- It breaks you up
- It fractures you
- It kills you
- It slays you
- It tickles your funnybone
- Keep someone in stitches
- Laugh 'til you cry
- Roar with laughter
- Screamingly funny
- See the humor in something
- Thigh-slapper
- Think it's uproarious

**OR CAN BE DESCRIBED AS:**

- The best medicine

# IT'S NOT FUNNY

## WHEN IT'S NOT FUNNY, IT'S:

No Joke, Not a Laughing Matter, Serious as a Heart Attack.

## AND CAN BE CHARACTERIZED BY THE FOLLOWING:

- Don't try to laugh it off
- Get serious
- Go ahead—amuse yourself at my expense
- I really mean it—it's not a game
- I see no humor in it
- I'm not kidding
- I'm not trying to entertain you
- It's as funny as a crutch
- It's not meant to be amusing
- I've never been more serious in my life
- Knock off the laughs
- Quit clowning about it
- Quit horsing around
- Stop acting like a hyena
- What's so funny?
- Wipe that smile off your face
- You'd better believe it
- You'll be laughing on the other side of your face

## OR CAN BE DESCRIBED AS:

- Serious business

# II
# BODY TYPES

# LEAN AND LITHE PEOPLE

**LEAN AND LITHE PEOPLE ARE:**

Match Sticks, Skeletons, Skinny People, String Beans, Thin People, Toothpicks.

**AND CAN BE CHARACTERIZED BY THE FOLLOWING:**

- A stiff wind would blow him right away
- You can see right through him
- Can count his ribs from a mile away
- Can't see him when he stands sideways

- He can't cast a shadow
- My dog might bury him
- Resembles a match stick
- Wind might blow him away
- You can count his ribs
- You can see right through him

**OR CAN BE DESCRIBED AS:**

- A long drink of water
- A mere wisp of a thing
- A stretch
- A string bean
- Bony as a skeleton

- Lean and lanky
- Skin and bones
- Skinny as a rail
- Thin as a toothpick

# PERFECT PEOPLE

**A JUST RIGHT PERSON IS A:**

Babe, Bathing Beauty, Centerfold, Cover Girl, Dream-Boat, Goddess, Hunk, Model, Pin-Up, Venus, Ten, Adonis.

**AND CAN BE CHARACTERIZED BY THE FOLLOWING:**

- Beautiful hair
- Beautiful skin

- Built like an hourglass
- Everything's in its proper place

- Flawless face
- Flowing hair
- Groomed to perfection
- Looks like a Barbie doll

- Looks great in anything
- Not a hair out of place
- Sturdy as an oak

## OR CAN BE DESCRIBED AS:

- A living doll
- Muscular
- Perfectly built
- Perfectly proportioned
- Really put together
- Slim as a reed
- Solid—hard body

- Streamlined
- Strong
- Svelte
- Tall dark and handsome
- Well built
- Whistle-Bait

# OVERWEIGHT PEOPLE

## AN OVERWEIGHT PERSON IS A:

Blimp, Crisco Kid, Fleshed-Out, Heavy Weight, Hippo, Lard Butt, Roly- Poly, Two-Ton Tony.

## AND CAN BE CHARACTERIZED BY THE FOLLOWING:

- Acres and acres
- Blocks the sun
- Built like a brick house
- Built like a brick outhouse
- Can't see his shoes looking down

- Fat in the can
- Five-by-five
- Jiggles when he walks
- Needs to sit down

## OR CAN BE DESCRIBED AS:

- Big as a house
- Big as an elephant

- Broad in the beam
- Chubby

- Chunky
- Fat as a pig
- Full figured
- Heavy bottomed
- Heavy set
- Plump as a chicken
- Rotund
- Round as a ball
- Well endowed
- Well rounded
- Wide as a truck

# AGILE AND COORDINATED PEOPLE

## AN AGILE AND COORDINATED PERSON IS A:

Butterfly, Swan.

## AND CAN BE CHARACTERIZED BY THE FOLLOWING:

- As agile as a monkey
- As graceful as a swan
- As light as a feather on her feet
- Breezes along effortlessly
- Doesn't have two left feet
- Emits energy
- Floats like a butterfly
- Glides along
- Has a flowing rhythm
- Like a rippling stream
- Moves with effortless grace
- Never stumbles
- Symphony of movement

## OR CAN BE DESCRIBED AS:

- Charismatic
- Flowing
- Graceful
- Rhythm in motion
- Smooth as silk
- Sure-footed
- Synchronized

# AWKWARD PEOPLE

## AN AWKWARD PERSON IS A:

Brute, Bull in a China Shop, Clod, Klutz, Ox.

## AND CAN BE CHARACTERIZED BY THE FOLLOWING:

- Abounds in accidents
- Brute force and awkwardness
- Bumps into walls
- Can't chew gum and walk at the same time
- Can't get up without falling
- Can't put one foot past the other without tripping
- Dangles over things
- Flirts with disaster
- Gets in his own way
- Has more thumbs than fingers
- Lumbers along
- Puts his foot in the bucket
- Stiff as a board
- Stumbles around
- Trips over his own feet
- Trips over people
- Watch out!

## OR CAN BE DESCRIBED AS:

- All feet and elbows
- All thumbs
- Clumsy as an ox
- Creaky as an old mill
- Graceful as a hippo
- Liable to poke his own eye out

# THE ELDERLY

**THE ELDERLY ARE:**

Crones, Dirty Old Men, Fountains of Knowledge, Golden Agers, Grandparents, Grey-Beards, Living Historians, Matronly Ladies, Old Bats, Old Buzzards, Old Goats, Old Hags, Oldsters, Patriarchs, Retired Folks, Seniors, Senior Citizens, Silver-Haired Gentlemen, The Elderly, The Matured Generation.

**AND CAN BE CHARACTERIZED BY THE FOLLOWING:**

- Aging badly
- Baby-sitting grandchildren
- Bailing their children out of jams
- Basking in their setting sun
- Becoming grey-beards
- Enjoying their golden years
- Getting flabby
- Getting forgetful
- Getting senile
- Getting weather-beaten
- Going downhill
- Going to pot
- Going to the dogs
- Going to pieces
- Happy in their twilight years
- Hitting the skids
- In their second childhoods
- Looking their age
- Losing it
- Making crafts
- Old as Methuselah
- Old as the hills
- On the cane
- On the way out
- Over the hill
- Out of it
- Picking up the pieces for the chips off the block
- Put out to pasture
- Reaping the rewards of all they sowed
- Relishing the fruits of their labor
- Role models
- Rubbing on the Ben-Gay
- Showing their years
- Shuffling along
- Sitting on the park bench
- Slipping badly
- Slowing down
- Spending their children's inheritances
- Starting to creak
- Swallowing pills
- Tasting the joys of retirement
- Turning grey
- Visiting the doctor
- Wasting away
- Wised up too late
- Worldly wise

## OR CAN BE DESCRIBED AS:

- Crotchety
- Dried up
- Drooling
- Experienced
- Falling apart
- Hobbling along
- Limping

- Sagging
- Shriveling up
- Skin and bones
- Withered
- Wizened
- Wrinkled up

# THE BODY UNBEAUTIFUL

## AN UNBEAUTIFUL BODY IS:

Flawed, Geekish, Imperfect, Ugly, Weird.

## AND CAN BE CHARACTERIZED BY THE FOLLOWING:

- A bad hair day
- A lined face
- Bags under the eyes
- Bloated face
- Bony fingers
- Cauliflower ears
- Chrome dome
- Circles under the eyes
- Crow's feet around eyes
- Dribbles when he drinks
- Fat fingers
- Fat-in-the-can
- Gnarled hands
- Has jowls
- Has love-handles
- Humped shoulders
- Jelly-belly
- Jug ears

- Lard butt
- Looks jaded
- Looks like a beached whale
- Looks like a sack of potatoes
- Looks like a sack of wool tied in the middle
- Looks like a tub of lard
- Looks like death warmed over
- Looks like hell
- Looks like it was caught in the rain
- Looks like something the cat dragged in
- Looks like something the tide washed up
- Looks like the wrath of God
- Looks washed out
- Looks weather-beaten

- No chin
- Sagging body
- Skin and bones
- Stubby fingers

- Thunder-thighs
- Waddle when walking
- Washboard ribs
- Wrinkle-belly

## OR CAN BE DESCRIBED AS:

- Bald as an egg
- Banana-nosed
- Barrel-chested
- Beatle-browed
- Bleary-eyed
- Blubbery
- Bony
- Bow-legged
- Bottom-heavy
- Broad bottomed
- Broad in the beam
- Bulging out all over
- Buck toothed
- Bushy-browed
- Chicken-legged
- Crane-necked
- Cross-eyed
- Double-chinned
- Droopy-eyed
- Fat-ankled
- Fat-assed
- Fat-headed
- Fat-nosed
- Flabby-armed
- Flat-chested
- Flat-headed
- Flat-footed
- Hammer-toed
- Hippy
- Hunch-backed
- Jut-jawed

- Knobby-kneed
- Knock-kneed
- Liver-lipped
- Lop-eared
- Low-browed
- Lumpy
- Ostrich-necked
- Pale as a ghost
- Pigeon-toed
- Pimple-faced
- Pin headed
- Pinch nosed
- Pointy-headed
- Pot-bellied
- Puffy-eyed
- Pug-nosed
- Rat-faced
- Red as a lobster
- Red-eyed
- Round as a ball
- Round-shouldered
- Runny-nosed
- Scar-faced
- Scraggly-bearded
- Scraggly toothed
- Scrawny-necked
- Ski-nosed
- Skinny as a rail
- Skinny-legged
- Slack-jawed
- Spindly legged

- Square-headed
- Squatty
- Squinty-eyed
- Stoop-shouldered
- Toothless

- Toothpick-legged
- Weak-chinned
- White as a sheet
- Wrinkled faced

# III

# COMPETITION

# WINNING

## WHEN YOU WIN, YOU:

Ace It, Beat The Odds, Break The Tape, Come Out On Top, Cop The Prize, Get The Blue Ribbon, Get The Gold, Grab The Brass Ring, Grab The Trophy, Hit It Big, Hit The Jackpot, Make Out Like a Bandit, Make The Winner's Circle, Take The Cake, Take The Crown.

## AND CAN BE CHARACTERIZED BY THE FOLLOWING:

- Beat the pants off them
- Beat them all hollow
- Come away a winner
- Come in all by yourself
- Come up smelling roses
- Come out in front
- Eat up your opponents
- Earn your laurels
- Earn your wings
- Lap the field
- Lead the field
- Leave them at the starting gate
- Leave them in the dust
- Make it a one-man race
- Make them eat your dust
- Run away with the race
- Run off with the cup
- Run rings around them
- Run roughshod over them
- Run them into the ground
- Show them your heels
- Soar to victory
- Tear up the field
- Win by a country mile
- Win by a landslide
- Win by a mile
- Win by a nose
- Win going away
- Win hands down
- Win in a walk

## OR CAN BE DESCRIBED AS:

- Being top of the heap
- Cleaning up
- Creaming them
- Nosing everyone out
- Plowing them under
- Sinking the opposition
- Skunking them
- Smoking them
- Smothering them
- Steamroll the opposition
- Triumphing over all
- Trouncing them
- Wiping up the floor with them
- Zapping them

# IN A TIE

## WHEN YOU ARE IN A TIE, YOU ARE:

Even Steven, Neck and Neck, Nip And Tuck, Side By Side.

## AND CAN BE CHARACTERIZED BY THE FOLLOWING:

- Can't see daylight between them
- Not a bit of difference
- Not a step apart
- Six of one—half a dozen of the other
- Too close to call

## OR CAN BE DESCRIBED AS:

- Anybody's guess
- A photo finish
- A toss-up

# LOSING

## WHEN YOU LOSE, YOU:

Blow Your Chances, Bow To An Opponent, Come In Second-Best, Cry Uncle, Eat Someone's Dust, Fail Miserably, Fail To Make The Grade, Get Beaten To A Pulp, Get Bruised And Beaten, Get Destroyed, Get Eaten Alive, Get Humiliated, Get Knocked Silly, Get Shot Down, Get Skunked, Get The Tar Kicked Out Of You, Get Walloped, Get Washed Out, Get Whomped, Get Your Brains Beat Out, Get Your Butt Kicked, Get Your Come-Uppance, Get Your Head Handed To You, Get Your Hide Tanned, Get Your Wings Clipped, Give A Pitiful Exhibition, Go Down In Defeat, Make A Sad Showing, Meet Your Match, Meet Your Waterloo, Miss The Boat, Strike Out, Take A Clobbering, Take A Drubbing, Take A Whipping, Take It On The Chin, Taste Defeat, Throw In The Sponge, Throw In The Towel.

## AND CAN BE CHARACTERIZED BY THE FOLLOWING:

- A miss is as good as a mile
- At the tail end
- Back out
- Become an also-ran
- Bit off more than you could chew
- Bringing up the rear
- Couldn't cut the mustard
- Couldn't keep up
- Down for the count
- Dragging along behind
- Get run over
- Go down in flames
- Have your bell rung
- Knocked on your fanny
- Knocked out of the race
- Left behind
- Left in the dust
- Left licking your wounds
- Look bad
- Lose by a step
- Miss by inches
- Not even close
- Not in competition
- Not up to the task
- On the bottom looking up
- On the outside looking in
- One step behind
- Out of contention
- Out of the running
- Out of your league
- Over your head
- Overwhelmed
- Put in your place
- Quit in disgrace
- Quit in the stretch
- Run into a buzz-saw
- Run out of gas
- Shot your load
- Tailing behind
- Taken over the hurdles
- Took on more than you can handle

## OR CAN BE DESCRIBED AS:

- Beaten
- Humbled
- Laid low

# SURRENDER

## WHEN YOU SURRENDER, YOU:

Back Down, Back Out, Cave In, Chicken Out, Chuck The Whole Shebang, Cry Uncle, Dip Your Flag, Fall On Your Sword, Fall To Your Knees, Give Up The Ship, Haul Down Your Colors, Lay Down Your Arms, Pull In Your Horns, Take

A Dive, Throw In The Sponge, Throw In The Towel, Throw Up Your Hands, Wave The White Flag, Weasel Out.

## AND CAN BE CHARACTERIZED BY THE FOLLOWING:

- Collapse
- Crumble in a heap
- Eat dirt
- Jap out
- Knuckle down to someone
- Lie down
- Pack up and leave
- Quit cold
- Quit in the stretch
- Slink off and lick your wounds
- Whimper like a whipped puppy
- Whine and whimper

## OR CAN BE DESCRIBED AS:

- Crawling for mercy
- Defeated
- Groveling

# DEFEATED WITH HONOR

## WHEN YOU ARE DEFEATED WITH HONOR, YOU:

Gave It Your All, Got Trounced But Tried, Hung In There, Hung On Until The End, Kept Coming Off The Floor, Learned A Lesson In Defeat, Lived To Fight Another Day, Took It Like A Man, Took It Like A Trooper, Took Their Best Shots, Took Your Lumps, Went Down Swinging.

## AND CAN BE CHARACTERIZED BY THE FOLLOWING:

- Asked no quarter
- Believe there's no shame in honest defeat
- Faced up to it
- Faced the music
- Fought with your bare hands
- Gave as good as you took
- Kept coming back for more
- Standing tall in spite of it all
- Took it on the chin
- Took your medicine like a man
- Went down with the ship
- You can't blame a guy for trying
- You can't win them all

**OR CAN BE DESCRIBED AS:**

- Bloody but unbowed

## EXCEPTIONALLY GREAT

**WHEN YOU ARE EXCEPTIONALLY GREAT, YOU ARE A/AN:**

Ace, Block-Buster, Champ, Star, Titan, Virtuoso, Winner.

**AND CAN BE CHARACTERIZED BY THE FOLLOWING:**

- Beats all
- Can't be touched
- Have to see it to believe it
- It takes the cake
- Knock the wind out of them
- Knock them for a loop
- Knock their eyes out
- Leaves everything else behind
- Leaves them speechless
- Leaves tongues hanging out
- Makes heads spin
- Miles ahead of the rest
- No comparison
- No words to describe it
- Nothing else like it
- Out in front
- Staggers the imagination
- They can't believe their eyes

**OR CAN BE DESCRIBED AS:**

- A one-time thing
- A wow
- Beyond comparison
- Defy belief
- Fantastic
- Light years ahead of the rest
- Out of this world
- Sensational
- Superb
- Terrific
- The greatest thing that came down the pikeTops
- Unbelievable
- Unreal

# TO BECOME NOTICED

## TO BECOME NOTICED, YOU:

Attract Attention, Become The Center of Attention, Create A Stir, Create Chaos, Create Havoc, Cut A Fancy Figure, Cut Up, Disturb The Peace, Get On The Front Pages, Hog The Show, Kick Up A Fuss, Make A Big Impression, Make A Big Splash, Make A Big To-Do, Make A Loud Clamor, Make A Grand Entrance, Make A Scene, Make The Headlines, Make Waves, Make Your Presence Known, Project Yourself, Rock The Boat, Steal The Spotlight, Stop The Show, Stop Traffic, Take Center Stage, Upstage Everyone.

## AND CAN BE CHARACTERIZED BY THE FOLLOWING:

- Ahem
- Arouse someone's interest
- Ask for the floor
- Ask to be heard
- Ask to be recognized
- Become celebrity
- Become a legend
- Become a recognized figure
- Become famous
- Become infamous
- Become prominent
- Become well-known
- Become the focal point
- Catch someone's eye
- Create a nice impression
- Cut a wide swath
- Disrupt the quiet
- Establish a reputation
- Get everyone talking about you
- Get someone's ear
- Go down in history
- Give notice of your intention to resign
- Grab someone by the ear
- Have all eyes turn on you
- Have your name become a household word
- Have your name on the tip of everyone's tongue
- Have your picture posted in every post office
- Make a name for yourself
- Make a noticeable difference by your contribution
- Make them sit up and take notice
- Put your best foot forward
- Raise your hand
- Shatter the silence
- Stand out in the crowd
- Stand out in your field

## OR CAN BE DESCRIBED AS

- Attention seeking
- Being a loud-mouth
- Being a model of virtue
- Being a shining example
- Being as bold as brassBeing a scene stealer

- Being a scene stealer
- Being head and shoulders above everyone else
- Being the image of perfection

# IV
# CREATURE COMFORTS

# TO DINE

**WHEN YOU DINE, YOU:**

Break Bread, Brown-Bag It, Chow Down, Eat On The Run, Eat With Company, Feed Your Face, Fuel Up, Grab A Bite, Have A Bite, Have A Repast, Order Carry-Out, Pack A Lunch, Put On The Feed-Bag, Raid The Refrigerator, Throw A Steak On The Fire.

**AND CAN BE CHARACTERIZED BY THE FOLLOWING:**

- Believe to eat alone is to feed
- Dining in style
- Eat everything in sight
- Eat fast food
- Eat home cooking
- Eat hot dogs
- Eat junk food
- Eat like food's going out of style
- Eat plain food
- Eat to live
- Eat tube steaks
- Enjoy tid-bits
- Get a doggie-bag
- Have a belly wash (soup)
- Have coffee Have klatch
- Live to eat
- Wash it down with coffee
- Watch what you eat

**OR CAN BE DESCRIBED AS:**

- Doing lunch with someone
- Eating a square meal
- Getting a good meal under your belt
- Having a bite to tide you over
- Noshing
- Snacking
- Taking tea

# HEAVY EATER

## A HEAVY EATER IS A:

Big Eater, Chow-Hound, Hog, Horse, Pig, Scarfer, Wolf.

## AND CAN BE CHARACTERIZED BY THE FOLLOWING:

- Big on seconds and thirds
- Bolts his food
- Chows down
- Digs in
- Digs in up to his elbows
- Dives in
- Doesn't leave a crumb
- Doesn't stop long enough to catch his breath
- Eating is his favorite past-time
- Eats anything that doesn't bite him first
- Eats enough for an army
- Eats like a horse
- Eats us out of house and home
- Has a hearty appetite
- Has his head in the dish
- Inhales his food
- Is digging his own grave with his knife and fork
- Licks the plate clean
- Lingers over the dish
- No slouch behind a knife and fork
- Not bashful at the table
- Stows it away
- Wolfs his food

## OR CAN BE DESCRIBED AS:

- A hearty eater
- A heavy-weight

# LIGHT EATER

## A LIGHT EATER IS A:

Bird, Calorie-Counter, Choosy Eater, Dieter, Fussy Eater, Nibbler, Picky Eater.

## AND CAN BE CHARACTERIZED BY THE FOLLOWING:

- Dilly-dallies with food
- Doesn't eat enough to feed a canary
- Eats like a bird
- Lingers over the dish
- Nibbles at it
- Plays with food
- Picks at it
- Pushes food around on the plate
- Slips it to the dog
- Stares at food
- Studies every forkful
- Talks instead of eating
- Turns up his/her nose at food
- Wastes more than he/she eats

## OR CAN BE DESCRIBED AS:

- A feather-weight
- A light-weight
- A skinny minnie

# TO BED/TO SLEEP

## WHEN YOU GO TO BED/SLEEP, YOU:

Become Dead To The World, Call It A Day, Catch Forty Winks, Catch Some Z's, Count Sheep, Crash, Crawl Into Bed, Die, Doze Off, Get Some Sack Time, Get Some Shut-Eye, Go Out Like A Light, Hit The Pillow, Hit The Sack, Jump Under The Covers, Pass Out, Retire For The Night, Sack Out, Saw Wood, Snore Up A Storm, Snuggle In, Zonk Out.

## AND CAN BE CHARACTERIZED BY THE FOLLOWING:

- Collapse on the bed
- Cork off
- Counting sheep to fall asleep
- Drag yourself into bed
- Drift off into space
- Drift off to sleep
- Fall unconscious
- Flop on the bed
- Go to slumber-land
- Grab a nap
- Pop a sleeping pill
- Pound the pillow
- Sleep like a log
- You're asleep before the second leg is in the bed

## OR CAN BE DESCRIBED AS:

- Being in the arms of Morpheus
- Catching up on your rest

# TO WAKE / TO ARISE

## WHEN YOU ARISE, YOU:

Come To Life, Crawl Out Of Bed, Drag Yourself Out Of Bed, Greet The Dawn, Hit The Deck, Hit The Floor, Pop Up.

## AND CAN BE CHARACTERIZED BY THE FOLLOWING:

- Barely heard the alarm
- Bleary-eyed
- Can't stand the daylight
- Didn't sleep a wink
- Feel like you've been drugged
- Fresh as a daisy
- Had a good night's sleep
- Half-asleep
- Hitting the snooze button
- Open one eye
- Peer out of half shut eyes
- Raring to go
- Ready to face the world
- Slept like a baby
- Still half-asleep
- Stretch and yawn
- Throw off the covers
- Tossed and turned all night
- Up at the crack of dawn
- Up with the rooster
- Wide awake

## OR CAN BE DESCRIBED AS:

- Facing a new day
- Quitting the bed

# TOILET TIME

## WHEN YOU GO TO THE TOILET, YOU:

Check The Weather, Do Your Duty, Excuse Yourself, Find The Ladies' Room, Find The Mens' Room, Go Potty, Go To The John, Have To Call Your Broker, Have To Powder Your Nose, Hit The Restroom, Make A Pit Stop, Make A Rest Stop, Relieve Yourself, Sit On The Throne, Tinkle, Use The Accomodations, Use The Convenience Room, Use The Facilities, Use The Telephone, Water The Bushes.

## AND CAN BE CHARACTERIZED BY THE FOLLOWING:

- Got the runs
- Have the trots
- Make number one
- Make number two
- Powder your nose
- Puke
- Throw up
- Upchuck

## OR CAN BE DESCRIBED AS:

- Taking a necessary
- Visiting the necessary room

# SMALL AMOUNTS

## SMALL AMOUNTS ARE:

Bits, Dabs, Dots, Dribbles, Hints, Iotas, Ounces, Pinches, Shots, Shreds, Smatterings, Specks, Tads, Tastes, Touches, Trickles.

## AND CAN BE CHARACTERIZED BY THE FOLLOWING:

- A dab of color
- A dot on the map
- A dribble of rain
- A faint aroma
- A glimmer of hope
- A handful of visitors

- A handful of voters
- A hint of garlic
- A little bit of luck
- A petty crime
- A pinch of salt
- A shot in the arm
- A shred of proof
- A sketchy description
- A skimpy portion
- A slight chance
- A slight stutter
- A slim chance
- A smattering of applause
- A smidgen of confidence
- A speck of dirt
- A spot of brandy
- A tad off
- A taste of the good life
- A touch of class
- A trickle of blood
- A weak solution
- A whiff of blood
- A wisp of a lass
- An iota of common sense
- An ounce of prevention
- An ounce of pride
- Barely noticeable
- Hardly could feel it
- Hardly sufficient
- Scarce as hen's teeth
- Scratching the surface
- Shed a tear
- Sketchy
- The least of your worries
- The whisper of trouble
- Tip of the iceberg

## OR CAN BE DESCRIBED AS:

- Little bits
- Meager amounts
- Mere specks
- Skimpy portions
- Small potatoes

# NEW BEGINNINGS

## NEW BEGINNINGS ARE:

Births, Creations, Embryo Plans, Fresh Starts, Ideas, Introductions, Kickoffs, New Leafs, Opening Remarks, Opening Shots.

## AND CAN BE CHARACTERIZED BY THE FOLLOWING:

- A fresh coat of paint
- Coming to life
- Dawn of a new day
- First crack out of the box
- For the very first time
- From the get-go

- From starters
- Hatching a plan
- Hot out of the oven
- How it all got started
- Just off the press
- Open the door to discussion
- Opening shop

- Seeds of discontent
- Start off the whole shebang
- Starting from scratch
- Starting with a clean slate
- The beginning of the end
- The gleam in a father's eye
- When the world began

## OR CAN BE DESCRIBED AS:

- A brand new idea
- Square one

# DRIVING A VEHICLE

## WHEN YOU DRIVE, YOU:

Barrel Down The Highway, Bum Up The Road, Cruise The Town, Drive The Limit, Get Some Wheels, Gun The Engine, Kick The Engine Over, Open Up The Throttle, Put The Pedal To The Metal, Throw It Into High.

## AND CAN BE CHARACTERIZED BY THE FOLLOWING:

- Bear down on someone
- Beat the light
- Bum a ride
- Bum rubber
- Car pool with someone
- Close the gap
- Come to a dead stop
- Crawl in traffic
- Cut someone off
- Double park
- Drag with someone
- Drop someone off
- Exceed the limit

- Gas it
- Gas up
- Get a jump start
- Get caught in a speed trap
- Get in a traffic jam
- Give someone a lift
- Got four on the floor
- Hang a left
- Hit the brakes
- Jockey for position
- Jump lanes
- Make your own lane
- Need a boost

- Need a jump
- Pick someone up
- Pour on the coal
- Pull off the road
- Pull someone over
- Pull up at the light
- Ride bumper to bumper
- Ride someone's tail
- Rides the brakes
- Rock it out of snow
- Run a light
- Run on fumes
- Screech to a stop
- Slam on the brakes
- Start like a jack-rabbit
- Step on the gas
- Switch lanes
- Take a comer on two wheels
- Tailgate someone
- Weave in and out
- Zoom off

**OR CAN BE DESCRIBED AS:**

- Tank up
- Eating up the road
- Use a radar buster

# CONSERVING ENERGY

**WHEN YOU CONSERVE ENERGY, YOU:**

Do Nothing, Hang Loose, Lie Around, Laze Around, Loiter, Sit Around.

**AND CAN BE CHARACTERIZED BY THE FOLLOWING:**

- Act like a couch-potato
- Act like a lazy-bones
- Can't see any sense in doing today what you could put off
- Until tomorrow
- Don't move a muscle
- Enjoy the scenes
- Enjoy your day off
- Flop on the bed
- Get all stretched out
- Go cruising
- Refuse to do anything productive
- Sack out
- Smell the roses
- Waste time

**OR CAN BE DESCRIBED AS:**

- Being idle

# V
# LETTING LOOSE

# CAROUSING

## WHEN YOU GO CAROUSING, YOU:

Go Bar-Hopping, Go Galavanting, Go Off On A Spree, Go Off On A Toot, Go Out On The Town, Go Skylarking, Have A Night Out With The Boys, Hit All The Joints, Hit The Night Spots, Take A Whirl Around Town.

## AND CAN BE CHARACTERIZED AS THE FOLLOWING:

- Believe tomorrow will take care of itself
- Blow the budget
- Break all the rules
- Break loose
- Cup a caper
- Cut loose
- Dance the night away
- Eat, drink, and be merry
- For Auld Lang Syne
- For old times sake
- Forget your troubles
- Have a ball
- Have a blast
- Have a rollicking good time
- Have one for the road
- Jump the fences
- Kick over the traces
- Kick up your heels
- Leave your worries behind
- Let all hell break loose
- Let it all hang out
- Let the chips fall where they may
- Let the joy-bells ring
- Let your hair down
- Let yourself go
- Live for today
- Live it up
- Live with abandon
- Paint the town red
- Party, party, party
- Pull out all the stops
- Raise hell
- Raise your glass on high
- Revel
- Rock to the dawn
- Run amok
- Sing and be happy
- Tear up the town
- Throw off the shackles
- Trip the light fantastic
- Turn the town on its ear
- Wear a lampshade
- Whoop it up
- Wild and wooly
- Wine, women, and song
- Your night to howl

**OR CAN BE DESCRIBED AS:**

- Being a night owl
- Swinging
- Taking yourself out for a good time

# ON DRINKERS AND DRINKING

**WHEN YOU DRINK, YOU:**

Chug-A-Lug, Drink Everyone Under The Table, Drink The Bar Dry, Drink To Forget, Drown Your Sorrows, Get A Glow On, Get A Jag On, Get A Load On, Get Drunk, Get Half-Lit, Get Plastered, Get Sloshed, Get Smashed, Get Snookered, Get Soused, Get Tipsy, Guzzle, Have A Little Nip, Have A Snort, Have Some Suds, Hit The Bottle, Inhale A Few Brews, Take Your Whiskey Neat.

**AND CAN BE CHARACTERIZED BY THE FOLLOWING:**

- Bellying up to the bar
- Bending your elbow
- Blotto
- Bottoms up
- Carrying a load
- Down the hatch
- Dried out
- Drink bathtub gin
- Drink it straight up
- Drink rot-gut
- Drink white lightning
- Drunk as a lord
- Feeling good
- Fell off the wagon
- Get blasted
- Get bleary-eyed
- Get blind drunk
- Get bombed out of your skull
- Get cock-eyed drunk
- Get crocked
- Get drunk as a hoot owl
- Get drunk as a skunk
- Get hung-over
- Get loaded
- Get the D.T.'s (Delirium Tremens)
- Get the shakes
- Hair of the dog that bit you
- Half-shot
- Have a beer belly
- Have a chaser
- Have a morning after
- Have one on the house
- High as a kite

- In your cups
- Loaded to the ears
- Loaded to the gills
- On a bender
- On a toot
- On the bottle

- On the rocks
- On the wagon
- Put it on the tab
- Rum-pot
- Rummy

# PAYING THE PIPER

**WHEN YOU PAY THE PIPER, YOU:**

Hang Over The Commode, Have A Hang-Over, Have A Morning After.

**AND CAN BE CHARACTERIZED BY THE FOLLOWING:**

- Rummy-nose
- Seeing double
- Sloppy drunk
- Social drinker
- Souse
- Staggering drunk
- Stiff
- Stiff as a board

- Swore off
- Tanked up
- Take one for the road
- Tee-totaler
- Three sheets in the wind
- Took the cure
- Took the pledge

**OR CAN BE DESCRIBED AS:**

- Being a boozer
- Being a booze-hound
- Being a lush
- Being a sot
- Being a tippler
- Being a wino
- Wetting your whistle
- Blood-shot eyes
- Can't stand yourself in the mirror

- Don't want to look at another drink
- Driving the porcelain bus
- Got the shakes
- Have a big head
- Holding your head
- Need a hair of the dog that bit you
- Need an eye opener
- Never again

- On the wagon
- Saying, "I can't believe I did it."
- Stomach turning somersaults
- Swearing off for life
- Throwing up your innards
- Vow to dry out
- You're tossing your cookies

## OR CAN BE DESCRIBED AS:

- Driving the porcelain bus
- Singing the blues
- Praying to the porcelain God

# VI
# ETHICS OR LACK THEREOF

# CONCEALING INFORMATION

## WHEN YOU CONCEAL INFORMATION, YOU:

Bury It, Clam Up, Cloak It In Secrecy, Keep It To Yourself, Keep It Under Wraps, Keep Mum, Keep Your Mouth Shut, Keep Your Own Counsel, Sweep It Under The Rug, Zipper Your Lips.

## AND CAN BE CHARACTERIZED BY THE FOLLOWING:

- Act deaf, dumb and blind
- Act ignorant about it
- Don't break your silence
- Don't let on you know
- Forget you ever heard of it

- Hear no evil, see no evil, speak no evil
- Keep a poker face
- Keep a tight rein on your tongue
- Keep it on the Q.T.

## OR CAN BE DESCRIBED AS:

- Being a sphinx
- Being silent as the grave
- Stone-walling

# REVEALING INFORMATION

## WHEN YOU REVEAL INFORMATION, YOU:

Blow Someone's Cover, Blow The Lid Off A Caper, Blow The Whistle On Someone, Fess Up, Fink On Someone, Flap Your Lips, Let It Drop, Let It Slip, Let The Cat Out Of The Bag, Let Your Tongue Wag, Rat On Someone, Run Off At The Mouth, Spill The Beans, Spill Your Guts, Squeal On Someone. Keep it under lock and key Keep it under your hat Lock it away Lose your memory Mum's the word Never bring it up Play cloak and dagger Play dumb Play it close to the vest Put a lid on it Shroud it in mystery Sit on it Stone-wall any inquiry Swallow your tongue Wear a blank look

## AND CAN BE CHARACTERIZED BY THE FOLLOWING:

- Be a stool pigeon
- Blurt it out Come clean
- Crack under questioning
- Get it all out in the open
- Get talkative
- Hang the rap on someone
- Have a loose tongue
- Have diarrhea of the mouth
- Lay the blame on someone
- Leak it to someone
- Level with someone
- Nail someone to the wall
- Put the finger on someone
- Sing like a canary
- Spit it out
- Talk in your sleep
- Talk out of school
- Take the wraps off a story
- Telephone and telegraph
- Tell a woman
- Tell it like it is
- Tell the whole story
- Turn someone in

## OR CAN BE DESCRIBED AS:

- Finking
- Ratting
- Snitching
- Squealing

# AVOID DETECTION

## WHEN YOU AVOID DETECTION, YOU:

Go Underground, Keep A Low Profile, Keep Off The Beaten Path, Keep Under Cover, Hug The Wall, Lie Low, Sneak Around, Stay In The Background, Stay Under Wraps.

## AND CAN BE CHARACTERIZED BY THE FOLLOWING:

- Act low-key
- Avoid eye contact
- Avoid publicity and notoriety
- Avoid the limelight
- Come out under cover of darkness
- Conceal your identity
- Cover your tracks
- Don't make waves
- Don't rock the boat
- Hide behind a beard
- Hide from view

- Hide in the shadows
- Hold your tongue
- Keep out of sight
- Keep out of the newspapers
- Keep to yourself
- Keep your head down
- Keep your trap shut
- Pull the shades down
- Speak in hushed tones
- Stay behind closed doors
- Stay close to home
- Stay on the fringe of activity
- Stay out of the light
- Turn your collar up
- Use an alias
- Use a nom de plume
- Wear a false moustache
- Wear shades

## OR CAN BE DESCRIBED AS:

- Being invisible
- Hiding

# TO BE GOOD

## WHEN YOU ARE BEING GOOD, YOU:

Behave Yourself, Keep Your Nose Clean, Mind Your Manners, Mind Your P's And Q's, Play It Straight, Walk The Straight And Narrow, Wear A White Hat.

## AND CAN BE CHARACTERIZED BY THE FOLLOWING:

- Abide by the rules
- Act like a goody-two-shoes
- Avoid the pitfalls
- Don't cop out
- Don't fall from grace
- Don't listen for the siren call
- Don't sell your soul to the devil
- Follow the good book
- Keep a firm hand on the tiller
- Keep off the grass
- Keep your mind out of the gutter
- Keep your skirts clean
- Keep your word
- Know right from wrong
- Listen to your conscience
- Set a shining example
- Stand up for what's right
- Stay clean as a hound's tooth
- Stick to your guns
- Toe the mark
- Walk the line
- Watch your step
- Wear a white hat

## OR CAN BE DESCRIBED AS:

- Being a boy/girl scout
- Being a knight on a white horse
- Being a leader
- Being a model of virtue

- Being a straight arrow
- Being above reproach
- Being four-square
- Being the salt of the earth

# DOING THE JOB RIGHT

## WHEN YOU DO THE JOB RIGHT, YOU:

Do A Bang-Up Job, Do It By The Book, Give It Your Best Shot, Put Your Best Foot

## AND CAN BE CHARACTERIZED BY THE FOLLOWING:

- Forward, Watch Your Work.
- Bust your gut
- Bust your hump
- Dig your heels in
- Do a polished job
- Do a smooth job
- Do it lickety-split
- Drive yourself hard
- Get it all together
- Get moving
- Give blood sweat and tears
- Give it some muscle

- Keep a finger on the pulse
- Keep your nose to the grindstone
- Knock yourself out
- Lean into it
- Make every minute count
- Nail down the problem
- Put some snap into it
- Put your mind to it
- Run with the ball
- Stay at it until you lick it
- Show what you're made of

## OR CAN BE DESCRIBED AS:

- Being a beaver
- Hitting the floor running
- Jumping in feet first
- Putting your shoulder to the wheel

- Shaking a leg
- Using some elbow grease
- Working up a sweat
- Working your finger to the bone

# DOING THE JOB POORLY

## WHEN YOU DO THE JOB POORLY, YOU:

Do A Half-Assed Job, Do A Slip-Shod Job, Do It Half Heartedly, Do It Helter-Skelter, Do It Hit Or Miss, Do It Like A Sly Fox, Do It Piece-Meal, Give It A Lick And A Promise, Slack Off, Slide By.

## AND CAN BE CHARACTERIZED BY THE FOLLOWING:

- Boot the ball
- Butter up the boss
- Do it by the seat of your pants
- Don't get your hands dirty
- Don't lift a finger
- Don't move a muscle
- Don't strain yourself
- Drag your feet
- Drag your heels
- Drop the ball
- Have no stomach for it
- Keep an eye on the clock
- Polish the apple
- Play it cool
- Play it slick
- Put your feet up
- Put your foot in a bucket
- Spin your wheels
- Straggle in
- Take your sweet old time
- Throw the bull
- Turn up your nose at hard work

## OR CAN BE DESCRIBED AS:

- Coasting
- Daydreaming
- Knocking off early
- Leaning on your shovel
- Putting up a front
- Screwing up
- Twiddling your thumbs

# VII
# INFLUENCE

# GENTLE PERSUASION

## TO PERSUADE GENTLY IS TO:

Coax, Con, Drop A Hint, Give A Soft-Sell, Give Friendly Advice, Give The Buddy Treatment, Make A Veiled Suggestion, Nudge, Promise The Moon, Paint A Rosy Picture, Soft-Soap Someone, Sweet-Talk Someone.

## AND CAN BE CHARACTERIZED BY THE FOLLOWING:

- Earning someone's confidence
- Filling someone's head with pipe dreams
- Flattering someone's ego
- Getting someone in a weak moment
- Handling someone with kid gloves
- Holding out a carrot
- Jolly someone along
- Laying it on thick
- Leading someone by the nose
- Lulling someone into a sense of security
- Making an offer he can't refuse
- Making someone feel comfortable
- Nudging him along
- Offering someone pie in the sky
- Playing on someone's sympathy
- Playing up to someone's vanity
- Putting a bug in his ear
- Putting a notion in his head
- Putting it in simple terms
- Selling him a bill of goods
- Slipping it to someone gently
- Stretching the truth
- Taking someone by the arm
- Taking someone by the hand
- Talking someone's ear off
- Talking impassionately to someone
- Talking to someone like a Dutch uncle
- Telling him it's for his own good
- Twisting someone's arm a little
- Weasel-wording someone
- Work on someone carefully

## OR CAN BE DESCRIBED AS:

- Buttering up someone
- Suckering someone
- Tempting someone
- Urging someone

# FORCEFUL PERSUASION

## TO PERSUADE FORCEFULLY IS TO:

Back Someone Into A Corner, Exert Your Influence, Get Someone Against The Wall, Get Up In Someone's Face, Have A Showdown, Kick Some Butt, Lay Down The Law, Make It Hot For Someone, Put The Pressure On Someone, Put The Squeeze On Someone, Talk Turkey To Someone, Threaten Someone, Turn The Heat Up On Someone, Turn The Screws On Someone, Work Someone Over.

## AND CAN BE CHARACTERIZED BY THE FOLLOWING:

- Bringing pressure to bear
- Drawing a line in the sand
- Getting someone by the short hair
- Giving someone a deadline
- Giving someone an either-or
- Holding his feet to the fire
- Insisting upon it
- It's not a matter of choice
- Laying it on the line
- Leaving someone no alternative
- Leaving someone no option
- Making someone like it or lump it
- No ifs, ands, or buts
- No more Mr. Nice Guy!
- Telling him to take it or leave it
- Threatening someone's life and limb

## OR CAN BE DESCRIBED AS:

- Arm-twisting
- Browbeating
- Bullying
- Insistence

# DOTE ON SOMEONE

## TO DOTE ON SOMEONE IS TO:

Baby Someone, Coddle Someone, Molly-Coddle Someone, Pander To Someone.

## AND CAN BE CHARACTERIZED BY THE FOLLOWING:

- Allowing someone to take advantage of you
- Allow yourself to be wrapped around a little finger
- Be a fall guy
- Be a patsy for someone
- Be someone's alibi
- Be someone's keeper
- Buy someone's excuses
- Carrying someone on the job
- Closing your eyes to someone's sins
- Covering up for someone
- Feel someone can do no wrong
- Going overboard for someone
- Letting someone run rough-shod over you
- Putting up with someone's shenanigans
- Rubber-stamping someone's lies
- Standing still for someone's wrongs
- Swallowing someone's insults
- Taking the blame for someone
- Taking the brunt of the blows for someone
- Taking the heat for someone
- Taking the rap for someone
- Tolerating someone's wrongdoings
- Turning the other cheek for someone

## OR CAN BE DESCRIBED AS:

- Worshiping the ground someone walks on

# DEMEAN SOMEONE

## TO DEMEAN SOMEONE IS TO:

Act Like He's Not There, Bad-Mouth Someone, Be Cool To Someone, Cut Someone Short, Dump Someone, Give Someone The Bum's Rush, Give Someone The Cold Shoulder, Humiliate Someone Publicly, Laugh In Someone's Face, Look Down On Someone, Make Fun Of Someone, Mimic Someone's Actions, Pay No Heed, Poke Fun At Someone, Put Someone Down, Ridicule Someone, Shove Someone Aside, Snub Someone, Talk Down To Someone, Tell Someone To Get Lost, Treat Someone Like A Buffoon, Treat Someone Like A Stooge, Treat Someone Like Dirt, Treat Someone With Contempt, Turn A Deaf Ear To Someone, Upstage Someone, Walk Out On Someone, Yawn In Someone's Face.

## AND CAN BE CHARACTERIZED BY THE FOLLOWING:

- Acting high and mighty with someone
- Calling attention to someone's faults
- Correcting someone in front of others
- Deflating someone
- Don't give them the time of day
- Elbowing someone out of the way
- Giving someone a blank stare
- Giving someone an icy stare
- Giving someone short shrift
- Giving someone the gate
- Having a big laugh at someone's expense
- Holding someone up to ridicule
- Ignore someone entirely
- Insult someone to his face
- Leaving someone talking to himself
- Letting someone cool his heels
- Looking down your nose at someone
- Lording it over someone
- Magnifying someone's failings
- Making a big deal of his errors
- Making a joke of his opinions
- Making a monkey out of someone
- Making someone a laughingstock
- Making someone grovel
- Making someone the butt of a joke
- Nit-picking someone's suggestions
- Pass over someone

- Patronize someone
- Playing someone for a fool
- Ridicule someone to his face
- Running rough-shod over someone
- Sending someone on a wild goose chase
- Showing someone the door
- Shuffle someone along
- Slamming the door in someone's face
- Smirking at someone
- Snickering at someone
- Taking advantage of someone
- Taking away someone's pride
- Talking behind someone's back
- Talking over someone's head
- Telling someone to go peddle his papers
- Telling someone to go soak his head
- Telling someone to go whistle
- Throwing someone a crumb
- Treating someone like a child
- Treating someone like a red-haired step-child
- Turning your back on someone
- Turning your nose up at someone
- Tweaking someone's nose
- Walking over someone like a doormat
- Walking past someone with your nose in the air
- Wiping your feet on someone
- Yanking someone's chain

## OR CAN BE DESCRIBED AS:

- Bullying
- Destroying
- Giving someone the big "I" little "u" treatment

# REPRIMAND SOMEONE GENTLY

## TO REPRIMAND SOMEONE GENTLY IS TO:

Call Someone On The Carpet, Chew Someone Out, Have A Talk, Slap Someone's Wrist, Take Someone Down A Peg, Take The Wind Out Of Someone's Sails, Talk Turkey, Tell Someone Off, Wake Someone Up To The Facts, Wise Someone Up.

## AND CAN BE CHARACTERIZED BY THE FOLLOWING:

- Calling someone's blunders to his attention
- Giving someone the facts of life
- Making things crystal clear
- Making someone know the score
- Making someone see the light
- Opening someone's eyes
- Pointing out the error of his ways
- Putting someone in his place
- Sitting someone down and talking to him
- Spelling out what's expected of him
- Straightening someone out
- Taking him by the ears and making him listen
- Talking to someone like a Dutch uncle
- Teaching someone the dos and don'ts
- Telling someone a thing or two
- Telling someone straight from the shoulder
- Telling someone where to get off

## OR CAN BE DESCRIBED AS:

- A pep talk
- A word of warning

# REPRIMAND SOMEONE FIRMLY

## TO REPRIMAND SOMEONE FIRMLY IS TO:

Bust Someone's Chops, Chew Someone Out, Climb All Over Someone, Come Down On Someone, Crack Down On Someone, Get Up In Someone's Face, Give Someone A Tongue Lashing, Hang Someone Out To Dry, Lambaste Someone, Lay Down The Law, Lay It On The Line, Put Someone Through The Wringer, Put The Fear Of God Into Someone, Raise Holy Hell With Someone, Read Someone Chapter And Verse, Read Someone The Riot Act, Shake Some Sense Into Someone, Take Someone To The Woodshed.

## AND CAN BE CHARACTERIZED BY THE FOLLOWING:

- Calling someone every name in the book
- Cutting someone off at the knees
- Climbing up one side of someone and down the other
- Coming down on someone like a ton of bricks
- Cutting someone down to size
- Cutting someone off at the knees
- Giving someone his come-uppance
- Giving someone what-for
- Hitting someone in the gut with it
- Hitting someone over the head with it
- Laying someone out
- Leaving no doubt in someone's mind
- Pinning someone's ears back
- Racking someone up
- Shaking someone up
- Taking someone by the shoulders
- Telling someone in no uncertain terms
- Telling someone no ifs, ands, or buts
- Tying a can to someone's tail

## OR CAN BE DESCRIBED AS:

- Commanding attention
- Commanding obedience

# REPRIMAND SOMEONE SEVERELY

## TO REPRIMAND SOMEONE SEVERELY IS TO:

Beat The Tar Out Of Someone, Box Someone's Ears, Break Bones, Crack The Whip, Kick Someone's Butt, Knock Some Sense Into Someone, Knock Someone From Pillar To Post, Lay The Stick To Someone, Lower The Boom On Someone, Nail Someone To The Wall, Put The Screws To Someone, Rack Someone Up, Rake Someone Over The Coals, Rap Someone's Knuckles, Take The Belt To Someone, Teach Someone A Lesson He'll Never Forget, Turning The Screws On Someone.

## AND CAN BE CHARACTERIZED BY THE FOLLOWING:

- Beating someone over the head
- Beating someone to a pulp
- Breaking every bone in some-one's body
- Burn it into someone's brain
- Cutting the legs out from under someone
- Hanging someone up by the ears
- Hitting someone up side the head
- Hitting someone over the head with it
- Holding someone's feet to the fire
- Knocking someone's head against the wall
- Knocking the starch out of someone
- Making someone wish he'd never been bom
- Tying a knot in someone's tail

## OR CAN BE DESCRIBED AS:

- Whipping up on somebody

# ADMONISH SOMEONE ANGRILY

## TO ADMONISH SOMEONE HOTLY IS TO:

Blister Someone's Hide, Boil Someone In Oil, Boil Someone In Water, Breathe Fire And Smoke At Someone, Bum Someone To A Crisp, Fire Someone, Flare Up At Someone, Fry Someone's Hide, Get Hot-Tempered With Someone, Get Sizzling Mad At Someone, Get Steaming Mad At Someone, Hold Someone's Feet To The Fire, Make Someone Walk On Hot Coals, Roast Someone, Set Fire To Someone's Britches, Warm The Seat Of Someone's Pants.

## AND CAN BE CHARACTERIZED BY THE FOLLOWING:

- Burning it into someone's brain
- Burning someone up
- Burning up at someone's antics
- Branding someone a liar
- Condemning someone to a fiery fate
- Cooking up a punishment for someone

- Finding someone too hot to handle
- Getting all heated up over someone
- Getting boiling mad
- Getting hot as hell with someone
- Getting hot on someone's trail
- Getting hot under the collar
- Giving someone a hot foot
- Giving someone a hot time
- Hot-foot it after someone
- Igniting someone's anger
- Letting the discussion overheat
- Letting someone stew
- Lighting a fire under someone
- Making it hot for someone
- Putting a match to someone's plans
- Preaching hell and damnation to someone
- Raking someone over the coals
- Sending someone's hopes up in smoke
- Singe someone's whiskers
- Smoking someone out of hiding
- Throw someone a hot potato
- Treating someone like a hot-head

## OR CAN BE DESCRIBED AS:

- Getting into a heated argument
- Getting into a hot dispute
- Spitting fire

# WARM UP TO SOMEONE

## TO WARM UP TO SOMEONE IS TO:

Develop A Warm Friendship With Someone, Greet Someone Warmly, Spark With Someone.

## AND CAN BE CHARACTERIZED BY THE FOLLOWING:

- A warm conclusion to a torrid and sizzling romance
- Being hot-to-trot to know someone
- Considering someone a hot number
- Feeling hot-blooded
- Feeling your heart melting
- Finding someone heart-warming
- Getting a hot date with someone

- Getting a hot idea about someone
- Getting hot as a firecracker
- Getting hot pants thinking about someone
- Getting yourself in hot water
- Giving in to a burning desire
- Having a hot time in the old town with someone
- Having a warm spot in your heart for someone
- Having the hots for someone
- Having your glasses steam up
- Making hot and heavy love to someone
- Proposing to someone in the heat of the moment
- Thinking of someone as a hot tamale

**OR CAN BE DESCRIBED AS:**

- Giving someone a hint of your warmth
- Thinking you're hot stuff

# TREAT SOMEONE SPECIAL

**TO TREAT SOMEONE SPECIAL IS TO:**

Be Someone's Buddy, Be Someone's Pal, Favor Someone, Give A Lot Of Lee-way To Someone, Give Someone A Break, Go The Extra Mile For Someone, Go Out Of Your Way For Someone, Handle Someone With Care, Handle Someone With Kid Gloves, Lay Out The Red Carpet For Someone, Make Over Someone, Make Provisions For Someone, Put Someone On A Pedestal, Treat Someone Gently, Treat Someone Like Royalty, Treat Someone Tenderly, Wrap Someone In Cotton.

**AND CAN BE CHARACTERIZED BY THE FOLLOWING:**

- Backing someone up
- Being someone's ally
- Being someone's confidant
- Bending over backwards for someone
- Bending the rules for someone
- Bolstering someone's ego
- Carrying the ball for someone
- Cutting someone a lot of slack
- Feeling for someone
- Giving of yourself to someone

- Giving someone a helping hand
- Giving someone a leg up
- Giving someone a lot of rope
- Going to bat for someone
- Having empathy for someone
- Looking out for someone
- Overlooking one's failings
- Propping someone up
- Protecting someone with your life
- Putting in a good word for someone
- Sharing the load with someone
- Standing behind someone
- Supporting someone
- Sympathizing with someone
- Taking pains in treating one
- Taking someone into your heart
- Taking someone under your wing
- Understanding someone
- Watching over someone

## OR CAN BE DESCRIBED AS:

- Extending yourself for someone
- Making allowances for someone
- Making exceptions for someone
- Making the way easy for someone
- Stretching the rules for someone

# TREAT SOMEONE COLDLY

## TO TREAT SOMEONE COLDLY IS TO:

Act Chilly Towards Someone, Be Cold And Calculating About Someone, Be Cold-Hearted Towards Someone, Be Frigid Towards Someone, Cold- Cock Someone, Freeze Someone Out, Give Someone A Cool Reception, Give Someone An Icy Stare, Give Someone The Cold Shoulder, Ice Your Relationship, Make Someone Shiver In Fear Of You, Quit Someone Cold, Snow Someone, Take Someone For A Sleigh Ride, Talk Cold Turkey To Someone, Treat Someone With Cold Contempt, Turn Someone Down Cold.

## AND CAN BE CHARACTERIZED BY THE FOLLOWING:

- Admitting someone's really a cool cat
- Becoming cool, calm and collected

- Catching someone cold
- Coldly throwing someone in the cooler
- Demanding cold cash from someone
- Don't give him a snowball's chance in hell with you
- Freezing someone in his tracks
- Giving someone a snow job
- Giving someone the hard cold facts
- He makes your blood run cold
- It'll be a cold day in hell before you help someone
- Letting someone cool his heels
- Letting your ardor cool for someone
- Letting your hostility cool off towards him
- Losing your cool dealing with someone
- Making a cool-headed decision about someone
- Put a freeze on his assets
- Someone puts you in a cold sweat
- Taking a cold hard look at someone
- Telling someone he leaves you cold
- Telling someone he's skating on thin ice with you
- Telling someone to cool it
- Throwing cold water on someone's ideas
- Turning someone out in the cold
- Waiting until you cool down before judging someone

## OR CAN BE DESCRIBED AS:

- Chilling someone out
- Freezing someone out
- Frosting someone

# BE CRITICAL OF SOMEONE

## TO BE CRITICAL OF SOMEONE IS TO:

Badger Someone, Bad-Mouth Someone, Be Someone's Judge And Jury, Belittle Someone, Blow Someone's Errors Out Of Proportion, Downplay Someone's Statements, Exaggerate Someone's Mistakes, Examine Someone's Every Word, Find Fault With Someone, Get On Someone's Back, Heckle Someone, Hold Someone Up To Ridicule, Hoot At Someone, Interpret Someone's Actions In The Worst Light, Jump All Over Someone, Magnify Someone's Faults, Make

A Federal Case Out Of His Every Mistake, Make A Joke Of Someone, Needle Someone, Pick On Someone, Pick Someone's Words Apart, Put Someone Down, Put Someone's Every Action Under A Microscope, Rake Someone Over The Coals, Read Into Someone's Statements, Run Someone Through The Mill, Scoff At Someone, Shoot Holes In His Ideas, Snicker At Someone, Step On Someone's Lines, Talk Behind Someone's Back.

## AND CAN BE CHARACTERIZED BY THE FOLLOWING:

- Attributing wrongs to someone
- Baiting someone
- Baiting the hook for someone
- Being a thorn in someone's side
- Being an albatross around his neck
- Being someone's nemesis
- Bugging someone
- Coming down on someone like a ton of bricks
- Criticizing someone's every move
- Cutting someone short
- Distorting someone's comments
- Dogging someone's footsteps
- Giving someone the bird
- Giving someone the raspberry
- Going out of your way to find fault with someone
- Hanging someone with his/her own words
- Holding someone to a rigid standard
- Hounding someone
- Imagining the worst about someone
- Laughing someone out of the room
- Looking over someone's shoulder
- Making a jack-ass of someone
- Making someone look foolish
- Making someone out to be a loser
- Panning someone
- Pick up on someone's slightest goof
- Poking fun at someone's comments
- Pulling apart what someone says
- Putting a monkey on someone's back
- Putting obstacles in someone's path
- Putting someone through the paces
- Putting words in someone's mouth
- Racking someone up
- Rolling your eyes at his comments
- Taking exception to someone's remarks
- Throwing cold water on someone's ideas
- Throwing someone's words back in his face
- Tripping someone up someone

## OR CAN BE DESCRIBED AS:

- Having no kind word for someone
- Making life miserable for someone
- Making snide remarks about someone
- Nit-picking at someone's statements
- Throwing barbs at someone

# NEGOTIATE FOR AGREEMENT

## TO NEGOTIATE FOR AGREEMENT IS TO:

Bargain In Good Faith, Bend A Little, Deal From The Top Of The Deck, Find A Middle Road, Find Some Common Ground, Get Off Your Pedestal, Give In On Something, Give Someone A Fair Shake, Give The Devil His Due, Hold Out An Olive Branch, Hold Out Your Hand, Humble Yourself, Leave A Door Open, Listen With Both Ears, Look At The Other Side Of The Coin, Meet Someone Halfway, Melt A Bit, Narrow The Argument, Open Your Mind, Reach Out To Someone, Refine Your Language, Smooth Out Differences, Soften Your Approach, Split The Difference, Sugarcoat Your Words, Tone Down Your Demands, Trade Off Demands.

## AND CAN BE CHARACTERIZED BY THE FOLLOWING:

- Admitting your shortcomings
- Backing off a little
- Biting your tongue
- Blinking at a failing
- Burying the past
- Burying the hatchet
- Coming down from the pulpit
- Coming down off your high horse
- Breaking the ice
- Coming to a meeting of the minds
- Don't be a know-it-all
- Don't be hard-nosed
- Don't hog the floor
- Don't talk down to him
- Finding the bone of contention
- Forgive and forget
- Giving a little

- Giving him a break
- Giving someone the benefit of the doubt
- Granting a point
- Half a loaf is better than none
- He who laughs last laughs loudest
- Keeping your cool
- Knocking off the rough edges
- Letting him blow his own horn
- Letting him get a word in edgewise
- Letting him save face
- Letting remarks fall off you like water off a duck
- Letting some remarks go over your head
- Letting some remarks pass
- Playing close to the vest
- Pretending not to hear all that's said

- Pulling in your horns
- Putting on a friendly face
- Putting yourself in his shoes
- Reading his body language
- Salve his ego
- Seeing things through his eyes
- Smiling, even when it hurts
- Stretching a point
- Swallowing your pride
- Taking a hard look in the mirror
- Thinking with your heart
- Throwing someone a bone
- Trying a new path
- Trying to see things his way
- Turning a deaf ear to some remarks
- Turning the other cheek
- Walking in his shoes

## OR CAN BE DESCRIBED AS:

- Coming down to earth
- Compromising
- Getting the whole picture
- Looking at the flip side

- Making an overture
- Picking up on suggestions
- Weighing some alternatives

# EXPRESS YOURSELF OPENLY

## TO EXPRESS YOURSELF OPENLY IS TO:

Bare Your Soul, Blow Your Cork, Expound On Your Views, Get It Off Your Chest, Give A Considered Opinion, Give One Man's Opinion, Hold Nothing Back, Impose Your Opinion, Lay It On The Line, Let It All Come Out, Let It All Hang

Out, Let Off Steam, Mouth Off, Open The Floodgates, Open Up To Someone, Open Your Mouth, Pop Off, Preach Your Philosophy, Pull No Punches, Put In Your Two Cents Worth, Reveal Your Innermost Thoughts, Run Off At The Mouth, Say What's Eating At You, Sound Off On Your Views, Speak For Yourself, State Your Case, State Your Convictions, Take The Floor, Tell It Like It Is, Tell It Straight From The Shoulder, Tell What's Troubling You, Think Out Loud, Throw Out An Observation, Unburden Your Concerns, Use A Bully Pulpit, Voice Your Opinions, Volunteer Your Opinion, Wax Eloquent On Your Ideas.

## AND CAN BE CHARACTERIZED BY THE FOLLOWING:

- Barging in on a discussion
- Being blunt
- Being straightforward
- Bending someone's ears on your point of view
- Butting in
- Button-holing someone to state your opinions
- Expressing your viewpoint
- Forcing your opinion down someone's throat
- Giving an unsolicited opinion
- Interjecting your comments
- Interrupting a conversation
- Inviting yourself into a discussion
- Jumping in with both feet
- Leaving no doubt on your views
- Letting everyone know where you stand
- Making a comment off the top of your head
- Making a snide remark
- Making comments from the sidelines
- Offering friendly advice
- Offering sage advice
- Poking your nose in on a private conversation
- Sharing your convictions with someone
- Speaking your mind
- Standing up and being counted
- Sticking your neck out
- Sticking your nose in where it doesn't belong
- Taking a stand on a subject
- Taking over a conversation
- Taking the stump
- Throwing in a comment

## OR CAN BE DESCRIBED AS:

- Giving your honest opinion
- Giving your point of view
- Letting your feelings pour out
- Making a frank comment
- Making your druthers known
- Making your position clear
- Making your position known
- Speaking your piece
- Telling it the way you see it

# INCREASING ROMANTIC INTEREST

## TO INCREASE ROMANTIC INTEREST IS TO:

Cast An Eye On Someone, Come On To Someone, Consume Someone With Your Eyes, Cozy Up To Someone, Drool Over Someone, Find Someone Attractive, Flip Over Someone, Flirt With Someone, Get A Yen For Someone, Get The Hots For Someone, Give Someone A Lingering Look, Give Someone A Second Look, Give Someone The Come-On, Give Someone The Eye, Go Ga-Ga About Someone, Go Into A Spin Over Someone, Like What You See, Make A Pass At Someone, Make A Play For Someone, Make Eyes At Someone, Make Your Move, Ogle Someone, Set Your Cap For Someone, Send Someone Signals, Size Someone Up And Down, Swoon Over Someone, Take A Liking To Someone, Take Someone's Measurements, Undress Someone With Your Eyes, Warm Up To Someone.

## AND CAN BE CHARACTERIZED BY THE FOLLOWING:

- A vision of loveliness!
- Becoming enamored of someone
- Becoming man and wife 'til death do us part
- Becoming putty in someone's hands
- Becoming someone's captive
- Becoming someone's slave
- Being attracted to him/her
- Being crazy in love
- Being nuts about someone
- Being smitten with him/her
- Being taken with him/her
- Can't eat or sleep because of someone
- Can't get him/her off your mind
- Can't live without him/her
- Can't take your eyes off him/her
- Dreaming about someone
- Falling for someone
- Falling head over heels in love
- Fantasizing about someone
- Feeling Cupid's arrow
- Finding him/her pleasing to the eye
- Getting bitten by the love bug
- Getting hitched
- Getting hooked on someone
- Getting hung up on someone
- Going bonkers over someone
- Having a happy ending
- Having your heart on fire
- He's the man of your dreams!

- Lie awake over someone
- Losing your heart to someone
- Love at first sight
- Makes your heart pound
- Pop the question
- Promise to love, honor and obey
- She's the girl of your dreams!
- She/he takes your breath away
- Showing your interest
- Taking notice of someone
- Tie the knot
- Time to make the big step
- Using body language
- Walk down the aisle
- Walking on air
- Walking two feet above ground
- Will sell your soul for someone
- You worship the ground he/she walks on
- You're at his/her beck and call
- You're wrapped around his/her little finger

## OR CAN BE DESCRIBED AS:

- Falling madly in love with someone
- Making overtures to someone
- Moving in on someone
- Setting a heart on fire

# VIII
# LIFE, HEALTH, AND DEATH

# RECEIVING UNEARNED
# GOOD FORTUNE

## TO RECEIVE UNEARNED GOOD FORTUNE IS TO:

Be Visited By A Leprechaun, Fall Into It, Find It Under Your Pillow, Find The Pot Of Gold, Get A Bonanza, Get A Windfall, Get It Through No Effort Of Your Own, Get It Without Moving A Muscle, Get It Without Sweat, Get Lucky, Have Fortune Smile Upon You, Have It Come Out Of The Blue, Have It Fall In Your Lap, Have It Fall Out Of The Sky, Have It Fall Your Way, Have It Handed To You, Have It Pop Out Of The Ground, Have Lady Luck Smile On You, Hit The Jackpot, Hit The Lottery, Reap Without Sowing, Uncork The Genie Bottle.

## AND CAN BE CHARACTERIZED BY THE FOLLOWING:

- Being in the right place at the right time
- Beyond your wildest dreams
- Come up smelling roses
- Everything comes to him who waits!
- Getting it when you least expected it
- Having it served up on a silver platter
- Having the Midas touch
- I believe in Santa Claus!
- Instant rich!
- Must have been living right
- Picking a four-leaf clover
- Picking it off the street
- Someone up there likes you!
- Striking oil
- Tripping over it
- Waking up and finding it there
- Yours to have, not to reason why

## OR CAN BE DESCRIBED AS:

- Being touched by a fairy wand
- Getting a lucky break
- Having a dream come true
- Having a fairy godmother
- Making out like a bandit
- Stumbling into it

## SICK

### TO BE SICK IS TO BE:

Aching All Over, A Basket Case, A Shell Of Your Former Self, Bandaged From Head To Toe, Breaking Out In A Cold Sweat, Burning Up With Fever, Clinging To Life, Down With Something Catching, Dragging Your Butt, Feeling Like You've Been Run Over By A Truck, Feeling Queasy, Feeling Ragged, Green In The Gills, Heartsick, In The Booby Hatch, In The Sick Bed, Laid Up, Loaded With Germs, Not Up To Snuff, Off Your Rocker, On The Bed Pan, On The Ward, On Your Death Bed, Runny- Nosed, Sick As A Dog, Slipping Away, Suffering Aches And Pains, Taken To The Bed, Under Doctor's Care, Under The Weather.

### AND CAN BE CHARACTERIZED BY THE FOLLOWING:

- As well as can be expected
- Being flat on your back
- Being stuck with needles
- Bleeding like a stuck pig
- Can't stand the sight of food
- Catching your death of cold
- Drowning in your own spit
- Every bone in your body aches
- Feeling like your head is about to explode
- Feeling peaked
- Feeling weak in the knees
- Going under the knife
- Got a bad ticker
- Got a bug
- Got the miseries
- Having a belly ache
- Having a coated tongue
- Having a headache that won't quit
- Having a nagging headache
- Having a sick tummy
- Having blood shot eyes
- Having hot flashes
- Having spots before your eyes
- Having the "Old-timers'" disease
- Having the runs
- Having the sniffles
- Having the trots
- Having watery eyes
- Having your cast autographed
- Having your life slipping away
- Hobbling on crutches
- In splints
- Just want to be left alone
- Limp as a wet rag
- Needing some TLC
- Needing your plumbing repaired

- Not your old self
- Off your feed
- Oozing life
- Patched up
- Popping pills
- Sick and tired of someone
- Sick to your stomach
- Sore to the touch
- The operation was a success
- Throwing up your insides
- Tongue tastes like cotton
- Wheezing like a locomotive
- Your mouth feels like the inside of a rubber boot

## OR CAN BE DESCRIBED AS:

- Having a pounding headache
- Having an upset stomach
- Looking like death warmed over

# TOUCHING DEPARTURES

## TO DEPART IS TO:

Be Six Feet Under, Be Stone Cold Dead, Bite The Dust, Cash In Your Chips, Croak, Get Carried Out In A Pine Box, Join The Angels, Kick The Bucket, Leave This Vale Of Tears, Make The Obit, Meet Saint Peter, Meet Your Maker, Pass On, Play A Harp, Return To Ashes, Return To Dust.

## AND CAN BE CHARACTERIZED BY THE FOLLOWING:

- Ashes to ashes
- Blown to bits
- Bought it
- Bought the farm
- Cold as a mackerel
- Cold in the ground
- Dispatched
- Dust to dust
- Eliminated
- Eradicated
- Erased
- Feeding the fishes
- Fried (Electrocuted)
- Getting shot down
- Getting shot down in flames (Aerial combat)
- Gone up in smoke (Cremated)
- Gunned down
- Have a neck-tie party (Hanged)
- Hit by a hit man
- Liquidated

- Long-gone
- On the bottom of the sea
- On the last round-up
- Out of this world
- Pushing up daisies
- Rubbed out
- Shark bait
- Shivved
- Shoveling coal (In Hell)
- Smoked
- Snuffed out
- Stretching a rope (Hanged)
- Taking the gas pipe (Suicide)
- Terminated
- Ventilated
- Wasted
- Wearing cement shoes
- Wearing wings
- Went under
- Whacked
- Wiped out

## OR CAN BE DESCRIBED AS:

- Being a dead duck
- Being dead as a doornail
- Being in the final sleep
- Going to the hereafter
- Knocking on the pearly gates

# CLOSE TO LEAVING

## TO BE CLOSE TO LEAVING IS TO:

Be On Death's Door, Be On Your Last Legs, Cling To Life, Hang By A Thread, Have One Foot In The Grave, Have The Devil Breathing Down Your Neck.

## AND CAN BE CHARACTERIZED BY THE FOLLOWING:

- Breathing your last
- Buying time
- Counting the minutes
- Feeling your life slipping away
- Giving your last gasps
- Just a matter of time
- Making peace with the Lord
- Not long for this world
- On the hit list
- On your way out
- Staring death in the face

## OR CAN BE DESCRIBED AS:

- Having a date with the grim reaper
- Looking over the edge
- Your time is up

# REFLECTIONS ON THE PAST

## TO REFLECT ON THE PAST IS TO:

Dig Up The Past, Drift Into The Long Ago, Go Back In Time, Live In The Past, Look Back On It, Mourn Your Lost Youth, Nurture Old Memories, Recall Yesteryear, Re-Live History, Re-Live The Past, Remember When, Resurrect The Past, Search Your Memory, Think Of Old Times, Walk Down Memory Lane.

## AND CAN BE CHARACTERIZED BY THE FOLLOWING:

- Bemoaning the passing of time
- Burying the past
- Hanging onto old dreams
- Let bygones be bygones
- The way it was
- There's no going back
- They don't make them like they used to
- Those were the days!
- Time and tide wait for no man
- Time marches on
- What's done is done
- When Grandpa was a pup
- When life was young
- When men were men and women were glad of it
- Wishing you had it to do over again
- Youth is wasted on the young

## OR CAN BE DESCRIBED AS:

- Living your life over
- Reaching back in your memory

# IX
# MENTAL STATE

# EAGER/ANXIOUS

## TO BE EAGER/ANXIOUS IS TO BE:

All Suited Up, An Eager Beaver, Busting To Get Going, Chomping At The Bit, Drooling In Anticipation, First Out Of The Starting Gate, Pawing The Ground, Raring To Go, Squirming On The Bench, Standing At The Ready, Straining At The Leash, Waiting For The Whistle.

## AND CAN BE CHARACTERIZED BY THE FOLLOWING:

- Bursting at the seams
- Can't contain yourself
- Can't sit still
- Counting the minutes
- Dying to get in on it
- Every muscle is twitching
- Hits the ground running
- On pins and needles
- Quivering with impatience
- Running out of patience
- Sweating it out
- Waiting to jump into the fray
- Wants it so much he can taste it

## OR CAN BE DESCRIBED AS:

- Being hot to trot

# VERY NERVOUS/OVER-ANXIOUS

## TO BE VERY NERVOUS/OVER-ANXIOUS IS TO BE:

A Nervous Wreck, All Keyed Up, At The End Of Your Rope, At Your Wit's End, Beside Yourself, Coming Apart At The Seams, Coming Unglued, Cracking Up, Falling Apart, Going Bananas, Going Berserk, Going Out Of Your Mind, Going Over The Edge, Going To Pieces, High Strung, In A Cold Sweat, In A Titter, Losing It, Nervous As A Long-Tailed Cat In A Roomful Of Mouse Traps, Ready To Blow, Stressed Out, Stretched To The Breaking Point, Tensed Up, Wound Tight As A Coil Spring.

## AND CAN BE CHARACTERIZED BY THE FOLLOWING:

- Biting your nails
- Breaking out in a rash
- Butterflies in your stomach
- Drumming your fingers
- Feel your heart pounding
- Feel your insides churning
- Feel your palms sweating
- Feel your stomach doing flips
- Having a dry mouth
- Having anxiety pains
- Having the shakes
- Having your stomach in knots
- Pacing the floor
- Pulling your hair out
- Shaking like a leaf
- Showing white knuckles
- Sweating bullets
- Talking to yourself
- Wearing out the carpet
- Wringing your hands

## OR CAN BE DESCRIBED AS:

- Antsy
- Fidgety
- Hyper
- Skittish
- Edgy
- Flipping your lid
- Jittery
- Twitching

# TIRED AND FATIGUED

## TO BE TIRED AND FATIGUED IS TO BE:

Beat, Beat Down, Bone Tired, Bushed, Dead On Your Feet, Dead Tired, Down For The Count, Dragging, Fizzled Out, Flagged, Out On Your Feet, Petered Out, Pooped, Ready To Collapse, Too Pooped To Pop, Washed Out, Whipped, Winded, Worn To A Frazzle, Worn Out, Zonked.

## AND CAN BE CHARACTERIZED BY THE FOLLOWING:

- Aching from head to toe
- All wound down
- All in
- Buckling at the knees
- Can't keep your eyes open
- Can't lift your feet
- Dragging your butt
- Every bone in your body aches
- Feeling your age
- Grinding to a halt
- Hanging on
- Lagging behind

- Limp as a wet rag
- Looking for a place to lie down
- Lost your zip
- Out of wind

## OR CAN BE DESCRIBED AS:

- Being on the ropes
- Being out of gas

# ENERGETIC

## TO BE ENERGETIC IS TO BE:

A Jumping Jack, A Live Wire, All Charged Up, Fired Up, Full Of Pep, Full Of Vim And Vigor, Full Of Vinegar, Wired Up.

## AND CAN BE CHARACTERIZED BY THE FOLLOWING:

- Bouncing
- Can't sit still for a minute
- Hopping up and down
- Hot as a firecracker
- In perpetual motion
- Psyched up

## OR CAN BE DESCRIBED AS:

- Bursting with energy
- Feeling your oats
- Having lots of zip

# HAPPY AND CONTENT

## TO BE HAPPY AND CONTENT IS TO BE:

Beside Yourself In Joy, Bubbling Over, Bursting With Happiness, Content As A Cow Chewing Its Cud, Crying Happy Tears, Ecstatic, Elated, Happy As A Kid In A Candy Store, Happy As A Kid With A New Toy, Happy As A Lark,

Happy As A Pig In Mud, In Clover, In Seventh Heaven, On Cloud Nine, On The Sunny Side Of The Street, Sitting On Top Of The World, Tickled Pink, Tickled To Death.

## AND CAN BE CHARACTERIZED BY THE FOLLOWING:

- At peace with the world
- Breathing rarified air
- Couldn't ask for anything more
- Enjoying the fruits of your labor
- Everything is aces
- Everything is coming up roses
- Everything is hunky-dory
- Everything is peaches and cream
- Floating on air
- Grinning from ear to ear
- Having the world by the tail
- Having your head in the clouds
- If this is a dream, don't wake me!
- It couldn't be better!
- Jumping in joy
- Not a care in the world
- Oh Happy Day!
- On a roll!
- Pinch me, I'm dreaming!
- Shedding tears of joy
- Sitting pretty
- Somebody up there likes me!
- This is as good as it gets!
- Walking two feet off the ground

## OR CAN BE DESCRIBED AS:

- Beaming happiness
- Being all-aglow
- Being pleased as punch
- Having the world by the tail

# SAD AND DEPRESSED

## TO BE SAD AND DEPRESSED IS TO BE:

Crying The Blues, Down At The Mouth, Down In The Dumps, Feeling Blue, In The Doldrums, In The Pits, Lonesome And Blue, On The Verge Of Tears, Singing The Blues.

## AND CAN BE CHARACTERIZED BY THE FOLLOWING:

- All alone in the world
- Can't face tomorrow
- Feeling crushed
- Feeling lower than a snake's belly
- Might as well be dead
- Life is the pits!
- Misty-eyed
- No one to turn to
- No will to live
- Nobody cares
- Not a friend in the world
- Nothing to live for
- Sad-faced
- Sitting alone in the dark
- Talking to yourself
- Tempted to end it all
- Where did I go wrong?

## OR CAN BE DESCRIBED AS:

- Being glum
- Looking like you lost your best friend
- Welling up in tears

# BECOME REJUVENATED

## TO BECOME REJUVENATED IS TO:

Come Alive, Come To, Get Cracking, Get Hopping, Get Some Zip, Get Your Act Together, Get Your Second Wind, Pep Up, Pick Yourself Up, Snap Out Of It, Snap To, Turn To, Wake Up.

## AND CAN BE CHARACTERIZED BY THE FOLLOWING:

- Coming to grips with it
- Getting a grip on yourself
- Getting off the pot
- Getting the lead out
- Getting with it
- Giving yourself a shake
- Open your eyes
- Shaping up
- Take hold of yourself
- Wake up and smell the coffee
- Wise up
- Zero in on it

## OR CAN BE DESCRIBED AS:

- Getting pumped up
- Getting recharged

# WORRIED ABOUT THE OUTCOME

## TO BE WORRIED ABOUT THE OUTCOME IS TO BE:

Antsy, Doubtful, Nervous, Skittish.

## AND CAN BE CHARACTERIZED BY THE FOLLOWING:

- Anything can go wrong
- Can't put my finger on it, but . . .
- How can I be sure?
- I don't have the whole story
- I feel funny about it
- I feel pressured
- I had better read the small print
- I hate to be negative, but . . .
- I have questions about it
- I shouldn't hang my hat on it
- I smell a rat
- I wouldn't stake my life on it
- I'd better check it out
- I'd better think it over
- I'm having second thoughts
- I'm not comfortable with it
- I'm not convinced
- I'm worried sick about it
- It doesn't seem kosher
- It doesn't sit well with me
- It doesn't sound right
- It gives me pause
- It smells to high heaven
- It's a gamble
- It's a pig in a poke
- It's a wild shot
- It's iffy
- I've got bad vibes about it
- I've got my doubts
- Leaving yourself wide open
- Let me sleep on it
- Letting down your guard
- Maybe I jumped too quick
- Not too sure
- Putting all my eggs in one basket
- Putting your neck in the noose
- Sight unseen
- Something is fishy
- Something is missing
- Something is not right
- Something is rotten in Denmark
- Something says I shouldn't

- Sounds too good to be true
- Sticking your neck out
- Taking a big chance
- There's a missing link

- There's got to be a catch
- There's no guarantee
- There's something behind it

## OR CAN BE DESCRIBED AS:

- What if I'm wrong?
- Being uncomfortable about the situation

- What if it bombs out?
- You can't be too sure

# TO WORRY EXCESSIVELY

## TO WORRY EXCESSIVELY IS TO:

Become A Basket Case, Fret And Fume, Get All Bent Out Of Shape, Get In A Stew, Let It Get To You, Let Yourself Go All To Pieces.

## AND CAN BE CHARACTERIZED BY THE FOLLOWING:

- Banging your head against the wall
- Breaking out in a rash
- Chewing your fingernails
- Feeling like you've been kicked in the stomach
- Getting your bowels in an uproar
- Have your head splitting

- Have your stomach churning
- Let it drive you to drink
- Let it keep you up nights
- Ready to throw yourself out the window
- Tearing your hair out
- Think about taking the gas pipe
- Wearing the carpet out pacing

## OR CAN BE DESCRIBED AS:

- Getting into the doldrums
- Getting your stomach in knots
- Going out of your mind

# REACTING TO MISFORTUNE

## TO REACT NEGATIVELY TO MISFORTUNE IS TO:

Blow A Fuse Or A Gasket, Come Unglued, Cry Doom And Gloom, Cuss People Out, Fall to Pieces, Get Bent Out of Shape, Get Down In The Dumps, Get Down-Hearted, Get In A Bad Mood, Go Ballistic, Go Into A Snit, Grumble And Groan, Kick The Slats Out Of A Door, Put On A Long Face, Raise Bloody Hell, Raise Cain, Raise The Dickens, Throw A Fit, Throw A Tantrum, Turn Sour On The World, Whine And Whimper.

## AND CAN BE CHARACTERIZED BY THE FOLLOWING:

- Banging your head against the wall
- Belaboring and berating everyone
- Bemoaning your fate
- Blaming everyone but yourself
- Complaining to high heaven
- Crying in your beer
- Crying your eyes out
- Cursing the fates
- Dropping out of sight
- Feeling sorry for yourself
- Getting down in the mouth
- Licking your wounds
- Not being fit to talk to
- Screaming at the top of your lungs

## OR CAN BE DESCRIBED AS:

- Bitching about it
- Going into hiding
- Hollering blue murder

# REACTING POSITIVELY
# TO MISFORTUNE

## TO REACT POSITIVELY TO MISFORTUNE IS TO:

Brush It Off, Charge It Off As A Bad Break, Climb Back Up In The Saddle, Dust Yourself Off, Chalk It Up To Experience, Grin And Bear It, Pass It Off As C'est La Vie, Pick Yourself Up, Put On A Stiff Upper Lip, Shake It Off, Square Your Shoulders, Start All Over Again, Take It In Stride, Try And Try Again.

## AND CAN BE CHARACTERIZED BY THE FOLLOWING:

- Accept that's the way the ball bounces
- It's the luck of the draw
- Come off the floor fighting
- Don't dwell on it
- It just wasn't in the cards
- Let it run off you like water off a duck
- Look to tomorrow
- Putting it in perspective

- Realize that's the way the cookie crumbles
- Say, "better luck next time"
- Say, "I complained because I had no shoes until I saw a man who had no feet"
- Say, "It could have been worse"
- You can't keep a good man down
- You can't win 'em all!

## OR CAN BE DESCRIBED AS:

- Counting your blessings
- Laughing it off
- Smiling through your tears

- Taking it like a man
- Turning the other cheek

# TRY TO FORGET AN
# UNHAPPY INCIDENT

## TO TRY TO FORGET AN UNHAPPY INCIDENT IS TO:

Avoid Thinking Of It, Become Oblivious To It, Block It Out Of Your Memory, Bury It, Chalk It Up To Experience, Close The Book On It, Close The Files On It, Close Your Mind To It, Cross It Off Your List, Crowd It Out Of Your Thoughts, Eliminate It From Your Mind, File It Away For Keeps, Get On With Your Life, Get Out From Under It, Give It Scant Attention, Let Bygones Be Bygones, Let It Die On The Vine, Let It Fade Away, Make It A Hazy Recollection, Make It A Vague Memory, Pass It Off, Pay It No Heed, Pay It No Mind, Push It In The Background, Put It Behind You, Put It In The Attic, Put It In The Back Of Your Mind, Put It On The Back Burner, Put It On The Shelf, Put It Out Of Your Mind, Put It To Rest, Relegate It To The Past, Scrub It Out Of Your Mind, Settle With It, Store It Among Dead Memories, Turn Your Mind To Other Things, Walk Away From It, Wash It Out Of Your Hair.

## AND CAN BE CHARACTERIZED BY THE FOLLOWING:

- Considering it a bad dream
- Considering it a dead issue
- Considering it a done deal
- Considering it a finished chapter in your book
- Considering it a thing of the past
- Considering it dead and buried
- Considering it over and done with
- Considering it signed, sealed and delivered
- Don't dwell on it
- Don't fret about it
- Don't give it a moment's thought
- Don't give it a second thought
- Don't let it bug you
- Don't let it cross your mind
- Don't let it get to you
- Don't let it haunt you
- Don't let it linger on your mind
- Don't look back
- Don't look over your shoulder
- Don't lose sleep over it
- Draw a blank on it
- Dump it
- Forgetting it ever happened
- Getting it off your back
- Ignoring it
- It's water over the dam
- It's water under the bridge
- Junk it

- Letting it die a natural death
- Letting it go by the board
- Letting it pass and be forgotten
- Letting it slide
- Pushing it to the recesses of your mind
- Scrap it
- Thinking of it in the past tense
- Waste no time thinking of it

## OR CAN BE DESCRIBED AS:

- Chucking it
- Dismissing it from your thoughts
- Erasing it from your memory
- Filing it in the circular file
- Putting it behind you
- Putting it in the inactive file
- Scratching it off your list
- Skipping it
- Turning your back on it
- Wiping it off the slate
- Writing it off

# FRIGHTENED

## TO BE FRIGHTENED IS TO BE:

Gripped In Terror, Horrified, Panic-Stricken, Scared Out Of Your Boots, Scared Out Of Your Socks, Scared Out Of Your Wits, Scared Silly, Scared To Death, Terrified.

## AND CAN BE CHARACTERIZED BY THE FOLLOWING:

- Frightened within an inch of his life
- Froze him in his tracks
- His hair turned white
- His heart nearly stopped
- His heart stood still
- His heart was in his shoes
- His heart was in his throat
- His heart was pounding
- His whole life appeared before him
- It was creepy, eerie, ghastly, weird
- Jumped out of his skin
- Made his blood run cold
- Made his skin crawl
- Made the hair on the back of his neck stand up
- Scared the living bejabbers out of him
- Scared the pants off him
- Sent shivers down his spine

- Shook him to the ground
- Turned him to ice
- Turned white as a sheet

## OR CAN BE DESCRIBED AS:

- Being petrified
- Having the hell scared out of you

# X
# MONEY

# FINANCIALLY INDEPENDENT

## TO BE FINANCIALLY INDEPENDENT IS TO BE:

Filthy Rich, Flush, In Clover, In The Chips, In The Lap Of Luxury, In The Upper Brackets, Living The Life Of Reilly, Loaded, Mr. Money Bags, On Easy Street, Rich As Croesus, Rolling In Dough, Sitting On A Gold Mine, Sitting Pretty, Top Of The Heap, Wallowing In Dough, Well Heeled, Well Off, Well-To-Do.

## AND CAN BE CHARACTERIZED BY THE FOLLOWING:

- Broke the bank
- Can buy you and me
- Eating high on the hog
- Got it made
- Got the Midas touch
- Has a fat wallet
- Has loads of mazuma
- Has lots of moolah
- Has money coming out of his ears
- Has more money than he knows what to do with
- Living it up
- Not a worry in the world
- Not counting pennies
- She's a rich bitch
- Sitting on top of the world
- Throwing money around

## OR CAN BE DESCRIBED AS:

- Being a fat cat
- Having megabucks
- Having money to bum
- Hitting the jackpot

# IN THE MIDDLE FINANCIALLY

## TO BE IN THE MIDDLE FINANCIALLY IS TO BE:

Bringing Home The Bacon, Building A Little Nest Egg, Comfortable, Holding Your Own, Keeping An Eye On Costs, Keeping The Wolf From The Door,

Paying The Bills, Putting A Little Aside, Putting Bread On The Table, Saving For A Rainy Day, Skimping On The Luxuries, Still Solvent, Stretching The Dollar.

## AND CAN BE CHARACTERIZED BY THE FOLLOWING:

- Hanging in there It's a living!
- Keeping body and soul together
- Keeping nose above water
- Keeping out of debt
- Making each dollar count
- Not hiding from the landlord
- Not wanting for the basics
- Not starving
- Skating by
- Skimping by
- Touch and go
- Watching the pennies

## OR CAN BE DESCRIBED AS:

- Making do
- Making ends meet
- Making it by the skin of your teeth

# FINANCIALLY EMBARRASSED

## TO BE FINANCIALLY EMBARRASSED IS TO BE:

Broke, Bumming A Dime, Busted Broke, Down At The Heels, Down On Your Luck, Down To Your Last Nickel, Eeking Out A Living, Facing Starvation, Flat Broke, Hard Up, In Debt Up To Your Ears, In Hock Up To Your Eyeballs, In Rags, In The Bread Line, Living From Hand To Mouth, Living On A Shoestring, On The Dole, Pinching Pennies, Poor As A Church Mouse, Scratching For A Living, Shabby Poor, Staring Poverty In The Face, Stretching A Dollar.

## AND CAN BE CHARACTERIZED BY THE FOLLOWING:

- Doesn't know where his next meal is coming from
- Hiding from the landlord
- Looking for a handout
- Grubbing a meal
- Not a dime to his name
- Hasn't got two cents to rub together
- Not a penny in his pocket
- Not a penny to call his own

- Not a red cent to his name
- On bread and water
- On his uppers
- On his way to the poorhouse
- Rolling change from his piggy bank
- Scrimping by
- Trying to keep body and soul together
- Trying to make a dollar out of 99 cents
- Trying to make ends meet
- Up against it
- Wallet's flat as a pancake
- Wouldn't recognize a dollar if he saw one

## OR CAN BE DESCRIBED AS:

- Being down and out
- Being in dire straits
- Being in the gutter
- Facing hard times
- Not having a pot to piss in
- Scraping the bottom of the penny jar

# GREEDY

## TO BE GREEDY IS TO BE:

Grubbing For Crumbs, Money-Hungry, Money-Mad, Wanting Everything In Sight.

## AND CAN BE CHARACTERIZED BY THE FOLLOWING:

- Has a bad case of want-itis
- His hand is always out
- Keeps coming back for more
- Latches onto leftovers
- Milks it for all it's worth
- Never satisfied
- Out for all he can get
- Socks away every cent
- Squeezes every penny
- Tries to get blood from a turnip

## OR CAN BE DESCRIBED AS:

- Being a grabber
- Being a penny-ante chiseler
- Being a scrounge
- Crying poor-mouth

# MAKE A PROFIT

## TO MAKE A PROFIT IS TO:

Come Up Winners, Have The Bucks Come Rolling In, Hit A Bonanza, Make A Bundle Of Dough, Make A Fair Return On Your Investment, Make A Fortune, Make A Killing, Make A Mint, Make A Pretty Penny, Make A Sizable Return, Make A Tidy Sum, Make Honest Bucks, Make Big Bucks, Rake It In, Reap Dividends, Strike It Rich, Strike Oil, Turn An Honest Dollar.

## AND CAN BE CHARACTERIZED BY THE FOLLOWING:

- Come up smelling like a rose
- Dollar signs are dancing in your head
- Got more money than you know what to do with
- Grab the brass ring Make money hand over fist
- Make more money than you ever dreamed of
- Make the cash register ring
- Money is coming out of your ears
- Ring up a profit
- Rolling in dough
- Stuff your pockets

## OR CAN BE DESCRIBED AS:

- Cashing in on a deal
- Cleaning up
- Getting a big payday
- Hitting the jackpot
- Making out like a bandit
- Sitting on a gold mine

# FAILED INVESTMENT

## A FAILED INVESTMENT IS A:

Busting, Cleaning, Fleecing, Hosing, Lost Gamble, Lost Wad, Ripping, Scalding, Scorching, Skinning, Wipeout.

## AND CAN BE CHARACTERIZED BY THE FOLLOWING:

- A fool and his money are soon parted
- Became a pigeon
- Bought a pig in a poke
- Bought the Brooklyn Bridge
- Cleaned me out of house and home
- Didn't even leave me car fare home!
- Flat as a pancake
- Fooled by smoke and mirrors
- Found all that glitters is not gold
- Got homswaggled
- Got in over your head
- Got it from the horse's mouth
- Got sheared like a lamb
- Got sold a bill of goods
- Got sold acres in a swamp
- Got sucked in
- Got taken every way but Sunday
- Got taken over the hurdles
- Got taken to the cleaners
- Had the wool pulled over your eyes
- In debt up to my ears
- Invested in a turkey
- It was fun while it lasted!
- It was too good to be true
- Led like a lamb to the slaughter
- Left holding fool's gold
- Left holding the bag
- Left me nothing but a bad taste in my mouth
- Lost my shirt
- Nothing left but the clothes on your back
- On my way to the poorhouse
- Picked clean to the bone
- Played for a patsy
- Poor as a churchmouse
- Poured money down a rat-hole
- Put it all on the line
- Robbed blind
- Sank a wad in it
- Selling apples on the street comer
- Snookered by a high-powered salesman
- Stripped bare
- Stripped clean as a whistle
- Swallowed a sales pitch
- Taken by a glib talker
- Taken down to my underwear
- Taken for a sleigh ride
- Taught me an expensive lesson
- They saw me coming!
- Threw good money after bad
- Took a bath
- Took a flier
- Took me for all I was worth
- Took me for everything down to my socks
- Watched my money go up in smoke
- Went broke
- Went down the tubes
- Went for broke
- Went for it, hook line and sinker
- Went for the pot of gold at the end of the rainbow

## OR CAN BE DESCRIBED AS:

- Being conned
- Being scammed

- Being shilled
- Kissing your money goodbye

# XI
# PERSONAL SPACE

# TO COME / TO ARRIVE

**WHEN COMING, YOU:**

Arrive, Bop In, Check In, Come Dragging In, Come Dressed As You Are, Come Rushing In, Come Sauntering In, Drop By, Drop In, Grace The Place With Your Presence, Make A Grand Entrance, Make An Appearance, Make The Scene, Make Your Presence Known, Pop In, Rush In Out Of Breath, Sashay In, Show Up Unexpectedly, Show Up, Show Up Uninvited, Sneak In Unnoticed, Stop By, Stop In, Swagger In.

**AND CAN BE CHARACTERIZED BY THE FOLLOWING:**

- Arrive in style
- Arrive in the nick of time
- Arrive on one's doorstep
- Arrive on the hour
- Arrive on the scene
- Arrive unannounced
- Be escorted in
- Come around
- Come back from the grave
- Come by invitation
- Come by your own invitation
- Come home
- Come in out of the cold
- Come in the back door
- Come on time
- Come out of the blue
- Come with bells on
- Crash
- Join the crowd
- Join the festivities
- Make it by the skin of your teeth
- Punch the clock
- Stick your head in to say hello

**OR CAN BE DESCRIBED AS:**

- Making an appearance
- Making an entrance

# TO GO / TO LEAVE

## WHEN GOING, YOU:

Blast Off, Bum Rubber, Bum The Retros, Cut Out, Go Lickety-Split, Go Like A Bat Out Of Hell, Hit For The Hills, Hit For The Woods, Hit The Gas, Hit The Road, Kick Up The Dust, Kick Up The Gravel, Leave A Trail Of Smoke, Leave In A Cloud Of Dust, Light Out, Make A Fast Exit, Make Tracks, Put The Pedal To The Metal, Put Your Butt In High Gear, Scat, Scram, Shift Into High, Show Someone Your Heels, Skedaddle, Split, Smoke Off, Step On The Gas, Streak Off, Take To Your Heels, Vamoose, Whip Past Someone, Whistle By, Zip Out, Zoom Off.

## AND CAN BE CHARACTERIZED BY THE FOLLOWING:

- Blowing town in high
- Breaking the speed records
- Busting out of the place
- Charging off like a rhino
- Cut out in a hell of a rush
- Firing up the engines
- Fly like the wind
- Get the lead out
- Going hell bent for election
- I'm out of here
- Make tracks out of there
- Move it
- Pick 'em up and lay 'em down
- Pour on the coal
- Scoot like a bunny
- Split in a cloud of smoke
- Step on it
- Take a comer on two wheels
- Take it on the lam
- Take off like a big bird
- Take off like a rocket
- Take off like a scared rabbit
- Tear-ass out of the place
- Tear up the road

## OR CAN BE DESCRIBED AS:

- Being in a rush
- Charging off
- Roaring off

# CLOSE ENCOUNTERS

## TO HAVE A CLOSE ENCOUNTERS IS TO:

Have One In The Palm Of Your Hand, Have One Under Your Thumb, Have Someone By Your Side, Have Someone In Your Pocket, Have Someone Under Foot.

## AND CAN BE CHARACTERIZED BY THE FOLLOWING:

- Another coat of paint and we'd have an albatross
- Back-to-back
- Eye-to-eye
- Eyeball-to-eyeball
- Hand-in-hand
- Head-to-head
- In bed with thieves
- Nose-to-nose
- Shoulder-to-shoulder
- Toe-to-toe

## OR CAN BE DESCRIBED AS:

- Being brothers under the skin
- Having a monkey on your back
- Having someone hanging over your shoulder

# RUSHING A RELATIONSHIP

## TO RUSH A RELATIONSHIP IS TO:

Come On Too Strong, Exceed The Bounds Of Propriety, Get Bold, Get Close, Get Out Of Line, Go Past The Limits, Go Too Far Too Quick, Move Fast, Overstep The Mark, Push Your Luck, Push Yourself On One, Put The Rush On Someone, Smother Someone, Swarm Over Someone.

## AND CAN BE CHARACTERIZED BY THE FOLLOWING:

- Become possessive
- Fast worker
- Getting carried away with yourself
- Getting grabby
- Getting out of hand
- Getting pushy
- Getting too close
- Having roving hands
- Making unwelcome advances
- Stepping over the line
- Taking advantage of one
- Taking liberties with someone
- Taking too much for granted

## OR CAN BE DESCRIBED AS:

- Getting fresh

# BECOME CURIOUS ABOUT ANOTHER'S AFFAIRS

## TO BECOME CURIOUS ABOUT ANOTHER'S AFFAIRS IS TO:

Get Nosey, Invade One's Privacy, Nose Around, Poke Your Nose In, Pry Into Someone's Affairs.

## AND CAN BE CHARACTERIZED BY THE FOLLOWING:

- Cock your ear
- Dying to find out
- Listening
- Putting your ear up to the wall
- Stretching your neck to see what's happening
- Tuning in on a conversation
- Watching one's every move

## OR CAN BE DESCRIBED AS:

- Being a nosey-body
- Sticking your nose in where it doesn't belong

# BECOME A NUISANCE

**TO BECOME A NUISANCE IS TO:**

Become A Wild Man, Butt In, Crash The Party, Create A Disturbance, Disturb The Peace, Elbow Your Way In, Foist Yourself On People, Follow Someone Around, Get In Someone's Hair, Get In The Middle, Get Out Of Hand, Get Rowdy, Go On A Rampage, Go Stark Raving Mad, Latch Onto Someone, Make A Scene, Offer Unsolicited Advice, Push Yourself On Someone, Shatter The Silence, Terrorize The Neighborhood, Volunteer Your Opinion, Weasel Your Way In, Work Your Way In.

**AND CAN BE CHARACTERIZED BY THE FOLLOWING:**

- Acting uncivilized
- Always want the last word
- Barging in on a conversation
- Become someone's shadow
- Breaking every rule in the book
- Defying authority
- Disrupting the peace and quiet
- Hanging on pne's every word
- Inviting yourself in
- Kicking over the traces
- Know it all
- Putting in your two cents worth
- Showing up unannounced
- Starting a riot
- Sticking to one like glue
- Taking the law into your own hands
- Tearing up the place

**OR CAN BE DESCRIBED AS:**

- Becoming an annoyance
- Being a buttinsky
- Being a clinging vine
- Being a fifth wheel
- Being a gate-crasher
- Being a hanger-on
- Being a Mr. In-between
- Being a thorn in one's side
- Running amok
- Running rampant

# XII
# PERSONALITY TYPES

# A SAD PERSON

**A SAD PERSON IS A:**

Constant Complainer, Depressed Person, Down In The Dumps, Gloomy Gus, Killjoy, Merchant Of Gloom, Miserable Person, Negative Person, Party Pooper, Pitiful Creature, Sad Sack, Wet Blanket.

**AND CAN BE CHARACTERIZED BY THE FOLLOWING:**

- Anxiously awaits his doom
- Believes the world owes him a living
- Bemoans his fate
- Bends your ear on his ills
- Bitches about life
- Blames his troubles on the world
- Cries in his beer
- Cries on someone's shoulder
- Complains to anyone who will listen
- Dwells on his misery
- Expects the worst
- Fears the unknown
- Feels sorry for himself
- Finds fault with everything
- Goes to bed feeling helpless and hopeless
- Has little faith in the world
- Imagines the worst
- Jumps to conclusions
- Kicks himself for past mistakes
- Laughs seldom
- Lives on pills
- Looks for sympathy or pity
- Makes dire predictions about every venture
- Makes mountains out of molehills
- Never raises the shades
- Opens his mail with dread
- Quits before he starts—for fear that he might fail
- Revels in his/her misery
- Recites each ache and pain
- Says "I told you so" when someone else's plans go awry
- Sees the glass as half empty
- Sees trouble lurking behind every comer
- Sings the Blues
- Spouts doom and gloom
- Throws cold water on fun
- Unloads his/her sorrows on the nearest listener
- Very depressed
- Wallows in his/her grief
- Wears a cloud over his/her head

- Whimpers and whines
- Worries himself/herself to death

- You don't have enough sense to get out of the rain—according to him

## OR CAN BE DESCRIBED AS:

- Complaining
- Depressed
- Down in the dumps
- Gloomy
- Malcontented

- Miserable
- Negative
- Pitiful
- Unhappy

# A HAPPY PERSON

## A HAPPY PERSON IS A:

Fun Person, Joy To Be With, Live Wire, Mary Poppins, Positive Person, Sight for Sore Eyes.

## AND CAN BE CHARACTERIZED BY THE FOLLOWING:

- A laugh a minute
- Bubbling over with joy
- Couldn't care less about problems
- Devil-may-care attitude
- Does your heart good to be in his/ her company
- Filled with a zest for living
- Fit as a fiddle and raring to go
- Full of fun and frolic
- Full of pep
- Full of vim and vigor

- Happy as a lark
- Lets worry run off him/her like water off a duck
- Lights up the room
- Never a dull moment
- No time for aches and pains
- Not a care in the world
- Sees the glass as half full
- Spreads the joy around
- Takes things in stride
- The world is his/her oyster
- Wears a perpetual smile

## OR CAN BE DESCRIBED AS:

- An eternal optimist
- Happy go lucky
- The life of the party

# A GENEROUS PERSON

## A GENEROUS PERSON IS A:

Do Good, Giving Person, Good Samaritan, Philanthropist, Real Life Santa Claus, Real Soft Touch.

## AND CAN BE CHARACTERIZED BY THE FOLLOWING:

- Can't pass by a hand held out
- Can't say "no" to anyone
- Digs deep to contribute
- Generous to a fault
- Gives from the heart
- Gives until it hurts
- Goes out of his/her way to help
- Has a heart as big as a house
- Has a heart of gold
- His/her wallet is always out
- Lives "It's better to give than to receive"
- Never met an unworthy cause
- Whatever he/she has is yours
- Would give one the food off his/her table
- Would give you the shirt off his/ her back
- Would share his/her last bite of food

## OR CAN BE DESCRIBED AS:

- All heart
- Everybody's friend in need
- His brother's keeper

# A SELFISH PERSON

**A SELFISH PERSON IS A:**

Heartless Character, Miser, Penny Pincher, Scrooge, Skinflint, Tightwad.

**AND CAN BE CHARACTERIZED BY THE FOLLOWING:**

- As cold as ice
- Cares only for Number One
- Chintzy
- Close with a dollar Conceited
- Cringes to think of paying
- Has a heart of stone
- Hoards his money
- Selfish with a capital "S"
- Squeezes a nickel 'til the Indian rides the buffalo's back
- Still has the first dollar he ever earned
- Tight with a buck
- When he/she takes out his/her wallet moths fly out
- Won't part with a dime
- Wouldn't give you the time of day

**OR CAN BE DESCRIBED AS:**

- Self-indulgent
- Self-obsessed
- Stingy
- Tight-fisted
- Self-centered

# A SPENDTHRIFT

**A SPENDTHRIFT IS A:**

Loose Goose, Prodigal Spender, Profligate, Squanderer.

**AND CAN BE CHARACTERIZED BY THE FOLLOWING:**

- Blows his wad
- Blows the bankroll
- Buys everything in sight
- Can't hold onto a dime

- Doesn't know the value of money
- Fritters away his money
- Foolish—a fool and his money are soon parted
- Goes through money like water
- Has champagne tastes on a beer income
- Has no head for money
- Lives "easy come—easy go"
- Money burns a hole in his pocket
- Money slips through his fingers like water in a sieve
- Spends it before he earns it
- Spends money like it's going out of style
- Thinks money grows on trees
- Throws money around

## OR CAN BE DESCRIBED AS:

- The last of the big spenders

# ORDINARY PEOPLE

## ORDINARY PEOPLE ARE:

Bread Winners, Consumers, Customers, Country Folk, Down Home Folks, Garden Variety Folks, Good Old What's His Names, Grass Roots People, Harry Homeowners, Joe Blows, John and Jane Does, Law-Abiding Citizens, Ordinary Joes, Plain Folks, Regular Guys, Run Of The Mill People, Run Of The Mine People, Rustics, Rubes, Simple Folk, The Average Family, The Average Individual, The Common Man, The Common People, The Face In The Crowd, The General Population, The General Public, The Man In The Street, The Middle Class, The Ordinary Citizen, The Public At Large, The Public Taken As A Whole, The Taxpayer, The Voting Public, The Working Class, The Private Citizen, Wage Earners.

## AND CAN BE CHARACTERIZED BY THE FOLLOWING:

- Are employed
- Are drivers and motorists
- Buy from catalogs
- Do their own housework
- Dwell in city or country
- Family oriented
- Follow the crowd
- Have in-laws and relatives

- Home-makers
- Keep up with the Joneses
- Know how to fix their own cars and plumbing
- Law-abiding
- Law enforcement people
- Live in fear of shut-downs and layoffs
- Love their families
- Make house a home
- Marital status varies from married to live-ins to single
- Pay taxes
- Plan and prepare their own holiday dinners
- Pump their own gas
- Salaried working mothers
- Send the children to public schools
- Send the children to daycare centers and babysitters
- Senior citizens
- Shop at Walmart and Kmart
- Single parents
- Sports nuts and fans
- Take care of their own business
- Teens
- They are the business establishment: shop-keepers and tradesmen
- Thirty-somethings
- Try to stay afloat
- Vote
- Walk with the pack
- Wash their own cars
- Working men
- Young adults

## OR CAN BE DESCRIBED AS:

- A dime a dozen
- Commonplace

# RICH PEOPLE

## RICH PEOPLE ARE:

Aristocrats, Entertainers, High Society, Sports Figures, The Elite, The Filthy Rich, The Privileged, The Rich and Famous, The Upper Class, The Upper Crust, The Well-To-Do.

## AND CAN BE CHARACTERIZED BY THE FOLLOWING:

- Are people with all that money can buy
- Born with a silver spoon in their mouths

- Can afford anything their heart desires
- Globe trotters
- Have more than they know what to do with
- Have access to plastic surgeons
- Have a maid, butler, housekeeper, and chauffeur
- Have a personal trainer
- Live off interest
- Make more money in a week than the common man sees in a year
- Never have to spend a principal sum
- Own more than one residence
- Party frequently
- Play the stock market
- Send the children to private schools
- Travel frequently
- Vacation any time they get the urge
- Work hard to maintain their image

## OR CAN BE DESCRIBED AS:

- The cream of the crop
- The lucky sperm club

## POOR PEOPLE

### POOR PEOPLE ARE:

Bums, Dependents, Drifters, Hobos, Idlers, Knights Of The Road, Low Brows, Low Lifes, Lower Class, Impoverished, Indigents, Loafers, Pedestrians, Street People, Tramps, The Criminal Element, The Down- and-Outers, The Needy, The Underprivileged, The Unemployed, Winos.

### AND CAN BE CHARACTERIZED BY THE FOLLOWING:

- Count pennies
- Don't feel quite human
- Feel like bums
- Have very little self-esteem
- Lack medical and dental care
- Look for a place to stay
- Look for a place to sleep
- Make every nickel count
- Marvel at others' wealth
- Stand in lines for assistance
- Visit the Unemployment Office

- Visit the Welfare Office
- Wash up in public restrooms and gas stations
- Wonder how to extricate themselves from the situation
- Wonder where their next meal is coming from

## OR CAN BE DESCRIBED AS:

- Broke
- Down and out
- Flat busted In Queer Street

# A SUPER PERSON

## A SUPER PERSON IS A:

Bom Leader, Natural Leader, Natural Talent, Paragon Of Virtue, Prince Of A Fellow, Real "Up" Person, Role Model, Shining Example, Winner.

## AND CAN BE CHARACTERIZED BY THE FOLLOWING:

- A cut above the rest
- A joy to be around
- A step ahead of the crowd
- Has a cool head
- Has a knack about things
- Has a magnetism
- Has a way with people
- Has all his ducks in a row
- Has an air about him
- Has his head on straight
- Has it all together
- Has the world by the tail
- Head and shoulders above the rest
- He or she is looked up to
- Knows his way around
- Knows where he's headed
- Lights up the room when entering
- No flies on him—will tackle anything
- No moss growing on him
- Nothing fazes him
- Nothing throws him
- On a pedestal
- Out in front
- Outstanding in his field
- People flock to him
- Sharp as a tack
- Smart as a whip
- Stands out
- Takes things in stride

## OR CAN BE DESCRIBED AS:

- An idol
- Mr. or Ms. Personality
- One in a million
- One of a kind
- The exception to the rule
- The envy of the crowd
- The leader of the pack

# A BORING PERSON

## A BORING PERSON IS A:

Blah Person, Bland Character, Blob, Cold Fish, Deadhead, Dead Pan, Downer, Drag, Flat Tire, Killjoy, Mealy-Mouth, Party Pooper, Poker Face, Wallflower, Wet Blanket, Wimp, Zero.

## AND CAN BE CHARACTERIZED BY THE FOLLOWING:

- Beats a story to death
- Beats the same old drum
- Drones on and on
- He turns you off
- Has a flat personality—is lifeless
- Has no spark
- Has you squirming in your seat
- Is drab as mud
- Is dull as stone
- Just takes up space
- Makes you yawn
- Needs a transfusion
- Needs some life put into him
- Puts a damper on things
- Puts you to sleep
- Rehashes the same old story
- Repeats himself like a broken record
- Sits like a bump on a log
- Will bore you to death
- Will bore you to tears

## OR CAN BE DESCRIBED AS:

- A dullard
- A stick in the mud
- A stuffed shirt

# AN UNPLEASANT PERSON

## AN UNPLEASANT PERSON IS A:

Bad Apple, Buttinsky, Fly In The Ointment, Gadfly, Grouch, Hanger-On, Hard-Nose, Horse's Ass, Know-It-All, Loud-Mouth, Mr. In-Between, Needier, Pain In The Neck, Wise-Apple.

## AND CAN BE CHARACTERIZED BY THE FOLLOWING:

- Can't get a word in edgewise with him
- Can't shut him up
- Carries a chip on his shoulder
- Causes an uproar
- Finds fault with everything
- Finds trouble
- Gets in the middle
- Gets in the way
- Grumpy
- Hard to get along with
- Has an answer for everything
- Has to have his own way
- Hasn't got a pleasant word for anyone
- He's a thorn in your side

- He's obnoxious
- Keeps the pot boiling
- Makes bad matters worse
- Makes the fur fly
- Nothing pleases him
- Nothing suits him
- Repeats himself
- Rubs people the wrong way
- Shoots off his guff
- Shoots off his mouth
- Stirs the pot
- Stirs up trouble
- Talks a blue streak
- Throws fuel on the fire
- Throws his weight around

## OR CAN BE DESCRIBED AS:

- An agitator
- An instigator
- A trouble maker

# AN UNTRUSTWORTHY PERSON

## AN UNTRUSTWORTHY PERSON IS A:

Cad, Con Artist, Creep, Crook, Double-Dealer, Rotten Apple, Scoundrel, Scutzball, Slimeball, Sticky Fingers, Thief.

## AND CAN BE CHARACTERIZED BY THE FOLLOWING:

- Crooked as a dog's hind leg
- Don't let him out of your sight
- Don't trust him as far as you can throw him
- Don't turn your back on him
- He'd cheat his own mother
- He'd steal the poor-box off the church wall
- He'll steal anything not nailed down
- He'll steal the eyes right out of your head
- He's bad news
- He's got sticky fingers
- Keep an eye on him
- Lies faithfully
- Not worth the powder it would take to blow him to hell
- Steals from right under your nose
- Watch your wallet
- Will rob you blind

## OR CAN BE DESCRIBED AS:

- The scum of the earth

# POMPOUS PEOPLE

## POMPOUS PEOPLE ARE:

Aloof Characters, Blue Bloods, Blue Noses, Cold Fish, Hard Noses, High-And-Mighty, Pompous Asses, Prides, Prudes, Ram Rods, Rich Bitches, Royalty, Stiff Necks, Stuffy Individuals, The Big Brass, The Big Wheels, The Big Wigs, The

Brass Hats, The Elite, The Landed Gentry, The Noveau Rich, The Rich and Famous, The Swells, The Upper Class, The Uppity-Ups, Up-Towners.

## AND CAN BE CHARACTERIZED BY THE FOLLOWING:

- Butter wouldn't melt in their mouths
- Breathe the ratified air
- Devoid of humor
- Don't mingle with the simple folk
- Drink their tea with raised pinkies
- Expect you to kiss the ground they walk on
- Faces would crack if they smiled.

- From the right side of the tracks
- On their high horses—look down their noses at others
- Pinch faced—straight laced
- Prim and proper
- Talk down to others
- Tight-assed
- Walk with a broom handle up their butt

## OR CAN BE DESCRIBED AS:

- Hoity-toity
- Holier-than-thou

- Stuffed shirts
- The powers that be

# AN ANNOYING PERSON

## AN ANNOYING PERSON IS A:

Bore, Buttinsky, Deadbeat, Gadfly, Hanger-On, Heckler, Know-It-All, Mr. In-Between, Needier, Nervy Character, Nosey-Body, Pain In The Ass, Pain In the Neck, Pest, Windbag.

## AND CAN BE CHARACTERIZED BY THE FOLLOWING:

- A nervy character
- A royal pain in the butt
- A thorn in your side
- Always has the answers

- Always in your face
- Annoying as hell
- Barges in at the worst time
- Bold as brass

- Bugs you
- Busts your chops
- Butts in on a conversation
- Can't get rid of him
- Can't turn around without bumping into him
- Can't turn him off
- Clings like a leech
- Constantly at your elbow
- Constantly repeats himself
- Constantly underfoot
- Crowds you
- Cuts you off while you're speaking
- Doesn't know his place
- Doesn't know when he's not wanted
- Doesn't know when to go home
- Doesn't know when to quit
- Dogs your footsteps
- Drives you crazy
- Drones on and on
- Gets in the way
- Gets in your hair
- Gets on your back
- Gets on your nerves
- Gets under your skin
- Gives you fits
- Hangs on your every word
- Has more chutzpah than good sense
- He's a deadbeat
- Irritates the hell out of you
- Irritates the life out of you
- Keeps coming back like a bad penny
- Leaves you no room to breathe
- Like a bad rash
- Like a weight around your neck
- Like an itch that won't quit
- Makes himself a nuisance
- Makes himself at home
- Moves in on you
- Nerve-wracking
- Parks on your doorstep
- Pesty
- Pokes his nose in where it doesn't belong
- Pushes himself on you
- Rehashes the same old stories
- Shows up uninvited
- Smothers you
- Sticks to you like glue
- Takes up space
- Talks you deaf dumb and blind
- Talks your ear off
- Tells you how to run your life
- Won't give you a moment's peace
- Won't take a hint
- Won't take "no" for an answer
- You detest the sight of him
- You have to step over him
- You wince to see him coming

## OR CAN BE DESCRIBED AS:

- A constant bother
- An irritant

# AN OVERLY-AMBITIOUS PERSON

## AN OVERLY-AMBITIOUS PERSON IS A:

Pushy Character, Schemer, Status Seeker, Super-Eager Beaver.

## AND CAN BE CHARACTERIZED BY THE FOLLOWING:

- Bears watching every minute
- Blind to the difference between right and wrong
- Bold as brass
- Brooks no competition
- Burns his bridges behind him
- Can't turn your back on him
- Claws his way to the top
- Climbs on others' shoulders
- Don't get in his way
- Edges his way in
- Gets what he wants by hook or by crook
- Got his cap set for it
- Has a "me first" attitude
- Has a one-track mind
- Has his eye on a goal
- Has his strategy mapped out
- Has no conscience
- Has no qualms about his ambition
- Has no regard for others
- Has the ethics of a stone
- He knows what he wants and how to get it
- He won't let up until he gets what he's after
- He'd sell you down the river
- He'll knife you in the back
- He'll run right over you
- He's a boot licker
- He's got his heart set on it
- He's hell-bent for election
- His ends justify his means
- Is not above lying and cheating to get his way
- Is one-way in all he does
- Kisses up to people
- Knows where he's headed
- Knows where his best interests lie
- Knows which side his bread is buttered on
- Lets the devil take the hindmost
- Like a fox in a chicken coop
- Never looks back
- Nothing discourages him
- Out for himself
- Out to make a name for himself
- Polishes the apple
- Promotes his own cause
- Pushes and shoves his way in
- Pushes his own agenda
- Pushes himself on people

- Puts himself first
- Rides another's coattails
- Runs over anyone who opposes him
- Runs roughshod over others
- Ruthless in his dealings
- Scrambling up the ladder
- Steps over bodies on the way up
- Takes a dim view of any competition
- There's no stopping him
- Thinks only of number one
- Uses cutthroat tactics
- Wants it so bad he can taste it
- Will stoop so low to get his way
- Won't let anything stand in his way
- Won't tolerate interference
- Worms his way into positions
- Would sell his soul to get what he wants

## OR CAN BE DESCRIBED AS:

- A boot licker
- A brown noser
- A conniver
- A hustler

# CHEATERS AND DECEIVERS

## CHEATERS AND DECEIVERS ARE:

Con Men, Dirty Dealers, Double-Talkers, Flim-Flam Men, Hoodwinkers, Liars, Manipulators, Scammers, Shafters, Slick Willies, Song-And-Dance Men, Story Spinners, Sweet-Talkers, Thieves.

## AND CAN BE CHARACTERIZED BY THE FOLLOWING:

- Bamboozle him
- Be a slick Willie
- Clean him out
- Clip him
- Con someone
- Cook up a scheme
- Deal from the bottom
- Double-talk him
- Ease your way into someone's confidence
- Fake him out
- Feed him a line
- Fleece him
- Flim-flam him
- Give him a snow job
- Give someone a song and dance

- Give someone the runaround
- Give someone the shaft
- Hold out on someone
- Hoodwink him
- Hook him
- Hose someone
- Lead him down the garden path
- Lead someone astray
- Lead someone down the primrose path
- Leave him penniless
- Lie through your teeth to him
- Lie to benefit yourself
- Load the deck against someone
- Make him a chump
- Make him a mark
- Make him a patsy
- Make someone a fall guy
- Manipulate someone
- Play cat-and-mouse with him
- Pick his bones
- Play the shell game on someone
- Play with loaded dice
- Pluck someone like a chicken
- Pull a fast one on someone
- Pull the wool over his eyes
- Put a spin on a story
- Put someone in the poor house
- Put something over on someone
- Reel him in
- Rip him off
- Rob him blind
- Run a con game
- Run a scam
- Sell him a bill of goods
- Sell him the Brooklyn Bridge
- Set someone up
- Shear him like a lamb
- Skin someone
- Slip something by him
- Slip something past him
- Snooker him
- Softsoap him
- Steal anything not nailed down
- Steal from under his nose
- Steal from widows and orphans
- Steal his eye teeth
- Steal the eyes out of his head
- Steal the gold out of his teeth
- Stick it to him
- Sting someone
- Strip him bare
- Strip someone clean
- Sucker him
- Sweet-talk someone
- Take him for a ride
- Take him for all he's got
- Take someone down to his socks
- Take someone in
- Take someone to the cleaners
- Take someone over the hurdles
- Take someone's last dime
- Take the bread out of his mouth
- Walk all over him
- Wipe him out

## OR CAN BE DESCRIBED AS:

- Wolves in sheep's clothing

# AN UNSOPHISTICATED PERSON

## AN UNSOPHISTICATED PERSON IS A:

Babe In The Woods, Back-Woodsman, Clod, Country Bumpkin, Diamond In The Rough, Farm Boy, Greenhorn, Hayseed, Hick, Rube, Small Town Boy, Wide-Eyed Innocent.

## AND CAN BE CHARACTERIZED BY THE FOLLOWING:

- A living example of "You can take the boy out of the country but you can't take the country out of the boy!"
- Awkward—all thumbs
- Blows his nose in his napkin
- Blows on his soup
- Can't make small talk
- Can't spell "etiquette"
- Dazzled by the glitter
- Doesn't fit in with the crowd
- Doesn't know the score
- Doesn't know which fork to use
- From the wrong side of the tracks
- Gawks at skyscrapers
- Gives himself away when he opens his mouth
- Grew up with the chickens
- Has a long way to go
- Has a lot to learn about life
- Has country manners
- Has no class
- Has no couth
- Has to be led around by the hand
- Has to learn the ropes
- Has two left feet
- Hasn't been exposed to the fast life
- In over his head
- Just off the boat
- Lacks the social graces
- Laughs at his own jokes
- Led a sheltered life
- Lights are on but nobody is home
- Like a deer staring at the headlights
- Like a fish out of water
- Like a kid in short pants
- Lost in the city
- Makes an ass of himself
- Needs sprucing up
- Not citified
- Not in the swing of things
- Not into the social whirl
- Not too suave
- Not up on the latest fads
- Not used to city lights
- Not used to the pace
- Not with it

- On the outside looking in
- Out of his element
- Out of his league
- Puts his foot in his mouth
- Raised in the boonies
- Raw material—needs polish
- Rough around the edges
- Rough-hewn
- Stands out like a sore thumb
- Still has straw in his hair
- Still wet behind the ears
- Straight from the farm
- Talks with food in his mouth
- Thinks "soup-and-fish" is a meal
- Traveling in the wrong circle
- Wide eyed

## OR CAN BE DESCRIBED AS:

- Coarse as grit
- Corn-fed
- Crude in his ways
- Fresh from the sticks
- Green as grass
- Short on refinement
- Uncool
- Unschooled in the ways of the world

# A WITHDRAWN PERSON

## A WITHDRAWN PERSON IS A:

Casper Milquetoast, Dead-Head, Downer, Drag, Face In The Crowd, Kill-Joy, Listener, Loner, Nerd, Nobody, Party Pooper, Shrinking Violet, Silent Sam, Timid Soul, Wallflower, Wet Blanket, What's-His-Name, Zero.

## AND CAN BE CHARACTERIZED BY THE FOLLOWING:

- Adds zilch to a conversation
- All elbows and thumbs
- Awkward in a crowd
- Awkward with the opposite sex
- Blends into the woodwork
- Can't carry on a conversation
- Closed-mouthed
- Dull as a stone
- Expects to be ignored and is
- Fears close contact with others
- Feels ill at ease around others
- Goes off by himself
- Hangs his head
- Has no opinion of his own
- Have to drag words out of him
- Hides from others at times

- In a vacuum
- Is low-key
- Just takes up space
- Keeps to himself
- Looks down at his shoes
- Misses out on the fun in life
- Never gets involved
- Never opens his mouth
- Not with it
- Not up on things
- Off in his own little world
- On the outside looking in
- Only speaks when spoken to
- Out in left field
- Out of place with people
- Out of the stream of things
- Prefers being alone
- Reads instead of socializing
- Shies away from company
- Shy to a fault
- Sits like a bump on a log
- Sits on his hands
- Sits on the sidelines
- Stays on the fringe
- Stumbles over words
- Swallows his tongue
- The cat has his tongue
- Timid soul
- Underrates himself
- Very quiet
- Wishes he had the gift of gab
- Worries too much about how he appears to others

## OR CAN BE DESCRIBED AS:

- A poor mixer
- Quiet as a mouse

# AN IMMODEST PERSON

## AN IMMODEST PERSON IS A:

Braggart, Braggadocio, Grandstander, Hot Dog, Know-It-All, Loud- Mouth, Party Animal, Pompous Ass.

## AND CAN BE CHARACTERIZED BY THE FOLLOWING:

- Admires himself in the mirror
- All puffed up with himself
- Avoids the simple folk
- Beats the drum for himself
- Believes his own resume
- Blows his own horn
- Bombastic

- Can't be accused of being bashful
- Cocky as a bantam rooster
- Comes on strong
- Compares himself to the best
- Doesn't have to be coaxed to talk about himself
- Eats up flattery
- Expounds on his virtues
- Fishes for compliments
- Flaunts his accomplishments
- Glories in his fame
- Goes out of his way to talk about himself
- Grabs the headlines
- Grabs the limelight
- Hams it up
- Has a high opinion of himself
- Has an ego big as a house
- Hogs the show
- Hot dogs it
- In love with himself
- Looks down on people
- Lords it over people
- Makes a big splash
- Makes his presence known
- Milks his exploits for all they're worth
- Not embarrassed by praise
- Not shy when relating his good points
- Plays the role
- Plays to the crowd

- Proud of himself
- Puffed up with his own importance
- Pumps himself up
- Pushes and shoves to grab the floor
- Puts on the dog
- Revels in the limelight
- Rides his high horse
- Rubs elbows with the Gentry
- Sets himself apart
- Shoots off his gruff
- Steals the scene
- Steps on everyone's lines
- Struts his stuff
- Struts like a peacock
- Swaggers around
- Takes all the credit
- Takes center stage
- Takes over the conversation
- Talks a good fight
- Thinks he's God's gift to women
- Thinks he's the cat's meow
- Thinks the sun rises and sets on him
- Thrives on attention
- Throws out his chest
- Toots his own hom
- Toots his own whistle
- Upstages everyone
- Walks with his nose in the air
- Waxes eloquent about his deeds

## OR CAN BE DESCRIBED AS:

- Big man on campus
- The center of attention

- The cock of the walk
- The life of the party

# A COOL-HEADED PERSON

## A COOL-HEADED PERSON IS A:

Cool Cat, Cucumber, Joe Cool, Level-Headed Person, Poker Face, Thick-Skinned Person.

## AND CAN BE CHARACTERIZED BY THE FOLLOWING:

- Acts cool as a cucumber
- Allows others to blow off steam
- Appears collected
- Appears unruffled
- Brushes it off
- Considers the source
- Controls his temper
- Controls the outcome by refusing to retaliate
- Counts to ten
- Deals with it
- Decides not to let it get his goat
- Displays an air of confidence
- Doesn't get bent out of shape
- Doesn't get ruffled
- Doesn't get stirred up
- Doesn't let it bug him
- Doesn't let it get to him
- Goes with the tide
- Grins and bears it
- Grits his teeth
- Hangs in there
- Has a high boiling point
- Has ice water in his veins
- Holds his tongue
- Holds his water
- Ignores it
- Is a cool cat
- Is laid back
- Keeps a level head
- Keeps a lid on his emotions
- Keeps a poker face
- Keeps a stiff upper lip
- Keeps a tight rein on his emotions
- Keeps his act together
- Keeps his balance
- Keeps his chin up
- Keeps his cool
- Keeps his head
- Keeps his head on straight
- Keeps his wits about him
- Knows it will blow over if he remains cool
- Lets it go over his head
- Lets it pass
- Lets it run off him like water off a duck
- Lightens up
- Loosens up
- Makes light of it
- Mentally considers all aspects of a situation

- Plays it cool
- Ponders the purpose of the exchange
- Realizes that getting him angry is someone's aim
- Refuses to be a pawn in someone's game
- Refuses to let someone pull his strings like a puppet
- Remains calm, cool and collected
- Rolls with the punches
- Shows no reaction to a taunt or accusation
- Simmers down
- Sizes up the situation
- Stands up to it
- Stays calm
- Takes it as it comes
- Takes it easy
- Takes it in stride
- Takes time to consider who said it and why
- Understands that some folks are not emotionally mature
- Waits it out

## OR CAN BE DESCRIBED AS:

- Unflappable

# A HOT-HEADED PERSON

## A HOT HEADED PERSON IS A:

Hot-Tempered Person, Red Head.

## AND CAN BE CHARACTERIZED BY THE FOLLOWING:

- Bites his lip
- Bites his tongue
- Clenches his fists
- Does a slow burn
- Feels he can't take it anymore
- Feels his blood boiling
- Feels his muscles begin to twitch
- Fights to control his temper
- Has beads of sweat on his brow
- Has knots in his stomach
- Has steam coming out of his ears
- Has veins in his neck standing out
- Has white knuckles
- Is holding back an explosion

- Is pushed to the edge
- Is ready to flip out
- Is red in the face
- Near the breaking point
- Patience wears thin
- Running out of patience
- Screams at people
- Sees red
- Seething inside
- Simmers
- Speaks before he thinks
- Stews
- Stifles a scream
- Temperature rises
- Yells

## OR CAN BE DESCRIBED AS:

- An angry person
- Ready to blow

# A PERSON WHO LOSES COMPOSURE

## A PERSON WHO LOSES COMPOSURE IS A:

Berserk Person, Blusterer, Cork-Blower, Fumer, Hothead, Lid Flipper, Lunatic, Rager, Raving Madman, Redhead, Spitfire, Steam-Blower, Wild Man.

## AND CAN BE CHARACTERIZED BY THE FOLLOWING:

- Acts like a wild man
- Bangs his head against the wall
- Bares his fangs
- Blood boils
- Blows a gasket
- Blows his cork
- Blows his mind
- Blows his top
- Blows steam
- Blusters and blows
- Can be heard in the next county
- Can't see straight
- Climbs the walls
- Comes apart at the seams
- Comes out swinging
- Creates a rumpus
- Creates an uproar
- Explodes
- Flails out in all directions
- Flares up
- Flies off the handle
- Flips his lid
- Foams at the mouth
- Freaks out
- Gets all bent out of shape
- Gets beside himself
- Gets beyond reasoning
- Gets boiling mad

- Gets burned up
- Gets fit to be tied
- Gets flaming mad
- Gets furious
- Gets hot as hell
- Gets hot under the collar
- Gets mad as a wet hen
- Gets purple with rage
- Gets red in the face
- Gets red hot
- Gets steamed
- Gets teed off
- Gets ticked off
- Gets up in someone's face
- Gets white knuckles
- Goes all to pieces
- Goes ape
- Goes bananas
- Goes berserk
- Goes crazy
- Goes insane
- Goes into a blind rage
- Goes off the deep end
- Goes over the edge
- Goes out of his senses
- Goes out of his skull
- Goes stark raving mad
- Goes straight up in the air
- Goes through the roof
- Goes wild
- Has conniption fits
- Has fire in his eyes
- His mind snaps
- Hits the ceiling

- Hollers bloody murder
- Is ready to commit murder
- Is ready to kill
- Kicks over the furniture
- Knocks out the walls
- Lashes out at people
- Loses control
- Loses his cool
- Loses his mind
- Makes a fool of himself
- Puts a fist through the wall
- Pulls his hair out
- Raises cain
- Raises holy hell
- Raises the roof
- Ready to strangle people
- Roars like a lion
- Romps around
- Screams like a Banshee
- Sees red
- Shakes a fist in one's face
- Spits bullets
- Spits fire
- Starts fuming and sputtering
- Starts throwing things
- Stomps like a raging bull
- Storms and rages
- Takes leave of his senses
- Takes off like a rocket
- Throws a temper tamtrum
- Turns livid
- Veins in his neck stand out
- Wants to jump out the window

## OR CAN BE DESCRIBED AS:

- Frenzied
- Unreasonable

# A PERSON WHO REGAINS COMPOSURE

**A PERSON WHO REGAINS COMPOSURE IS A:**

Fence-mender, Peace-maker.

**AND CAN BE CHARACTERIZED BY THE FOLLOWING:**

- Admits his own errors
- Becomes older and wiser
- Begins to see straight
- Begs someone's pardon
- Better luck next time
- Calls every knock a boost
- Calls it water over the dam
- Calls it water under the bridge
- Chalks it up to experience
- Charges it up to experience
- Comes down to Earth
- Comes to his senses
- Cools off
- Does his penance
- Doesn't beat a dead horse
- Doesn't cry over spilled milk
- Eats crow
- Faces up to his failings
- Gets back on track
- Gets on with his life
- Has egg on his face
- Is apologetic
- Kisses and makes up
- Lets bygones be bygones
- Lets it go
- Listens to reason
- Lives and learns
- Makes amends
- Makes up for the past
- Mends his fences
- Offers the olive branch
- Patches things up
- Pays the piper
- Picks up the pieces and goes on
- Plays mediator
- Pours oil on troubled waters
- Profits from past mistakes
- Puts it behind him
- Puts things back together
- Quits fussing
- Reaches a meeting of the minds
- Rebuilds from the ashes
- Says his mea culpas
- Says "What's done is done"
- Settles down
- Shares the blame
- Soothes one's feelings
- Starts with a clean slate
- Takes back his words
- Takes his lumps
- Undoes his wrongs
- Wipes the slate clean

## OR CAN BE DESCRIBED AS:

- Apologetic
- Compromising
- Forgiving

# A RECOGNITION SEEKER

## A RECOGNITION SEEKER IS:

Credit-Stealer, Drum-Beater, Ham, Hom-Blower, Role Player, Show Hogger.

## AND CAN BE CHARACTERIZED BY THE FOLLOWING:

- Angles for accolades
- Avoids modesty at any cost
- Beats the drums for himself
- Believes: when you've got it flaunt it; when you don't— fake it Blows his own horn
- Blows up his resume
- Calls attention to himself
- Doesn't act shy
- Doesn't hide his talents under a bushel
- Edges his way up to the front
- Elbows his way in
- Embellishes the truth
- Fishes for compliments
- Gets a kick out of being noticed
- Hams it up
- Hogs the show
- Horns in on things
- Is his own best agent
- Isn't bashful about speaking up for himself
- Justifies himself
- Knows how to play it
- Looks the part
- Makes sure he's noticed
- Never hides in the woodwork
- Often deceives
- Pads his credentials
- Plays the role
- Projects himself
- Pushes himself on people
- Puts a spin on his accounts
- Puts up a good front
- Slaps himself on the back
- Speaks in the first person
- Speaks up for himself
- Steals the limelight
- Steps forward
- Takes all the credit
- Takes center stage

- Takes every opportunity to be
- noticed
- Takes the floor
- Talks a good fight
- Throws his chest out
- Toots his own horn
- Volunteers his services
- Wants all the attention

## OR CAN BE DESCRIBED AS:

- An apple polisher
- A brown-noser
- The center of attention

# A STUBBORN PERSON

## A STUBBORN PERSON IS A:

Jack-ass, Stonewall.

## AND CAN BE CHARACTERIZED BY THE FOLLOWING:

- A tough nut to crack
- Can't be shaken
- Don't confuse me with the facts—my mind's made up
- Has a mindset
- Lets it in one ear and out the other
- Like talking to the wall
- Logic runs off him like water off a duck
- Made of stone
- No sense talking to him
- Not about to change his mind
- Turns a deaf ear to reason
- Unmoved by the facts
- Wants to have his cake and eat it too
- Won't budge an inch
- Won't listen to reason
- Won't meet you half way

## OR CAN BE DESCRIBED AS:

- Hardheaded
- Hard-nosed
- Immovable
- Impossible to convince
- Stubborn as a mule

# XIII
# SPEECH

# THE INCESSANT TALKER

## THE INCESSANT TALKER IS A:

Blabber Mouth, Chatterbox, Jabber-Mouth, Magpie, Marathon Talker, Nonstop Gabber, Talking Machine, Tongue-Wagger.

## AND CAN BE CHARACTERIZED BY THE FOLLOWING:

- Babbles without stopping
- Bangs our ears
- Bends your ears
- Blabs
- Blurts things out
- Can talk the ears off a brass monkey
- Can talk the ears off a mule
- Can talk the hind legs off a mule
- Can talk you blue in the face
- Can't keep his mouth shut
- Doesn't stop to catch his breath
- Drones on and on
- Goes on and on ad infinitum
- Goes on like a broken record
- Has something to say about everything and everyone
- He can talk his way out of murder
- His mouth is faster than his brain
- His tongue gets in the way of his wisdom teeth
- His tongue goes a mile a minute
- His tongue never gets tired
- Likes the sound of his own voice
- Lulls you to sleep
- Runs off at the mouth
- Never gives his tongue a rest
- Never runs out of words
- Never winds down
- Prattles endlessly
- Talks a blue streak
- Talks a mile a minute
- Talks like a parrot
- Talks to hear himself talk
- Talks up a storm
- Talks without thinking
- Talks your ear off
- There's no end to his opinions
- Will talk until he's blue in the face
- Will talk you deaf, dumb and blind
- You can't get a word in edgewise
- You get tired of listening

## OR CAN BE DESCRIBED AS:

- Being a motor mouth
- Having the gift of gab

# IDLE TALK

## IDLE TALK IS:

Chit-Chat, Gabbing, Gossip, Jibber-Jabber, Palaver.

## AND CAN BE CHARACTERIZED BY THE FOLLOWING:

- Chatting with someone
- Exchanging pleasantries
- Girl talk
- Guy talk
- Having a light conversation
- Making small talk
- Passing the time talking
- Talking about the weather
- Talking over the fence

## OR CAN BE DESCRIBED AS:

- Batting the breeze
- Chattering about nothing
- Chewing the fat
- Chewing the rag
- Chinning with someone
- Jawing with someone
- Shooting the breeze
- Shooting the bull
- Shooting the crap

# THE STRAIGHT TALKER

## THE STRAIGHT TALKER IS A:

Blunt Speaker, Straight Shooter.

## AND CAN BE CHARACTERIZED BY THE FOLLOWING:

- Comes right to the point
- Doesn't beat around the bush
- Doesn't hem and haw
- Doesn't honey-coat his words

- Doesn't mince words
- Doesn't pull his punches
- Doesn't spare your feelings
- Doesn't waltz around the subject
- Lays it on the line
- Leaves no doubt in your mind
- Lets the chips fall where they may
- Lets you know where he's coming from
- Makes a long story short
- Makes no bones about it
- Says it clear as a bell
- Says it like he means it
- Says it in plain English
- Says it right out
- Says what's on his mind
- Speaks from the heart
- Speaks his piece
- Speaks out on issues
- Speaks plain English
- Speaks up for himself
- Spells it out for you
- Talks sense
- Talks turkey
- Talks with an air of authority
- Tells it like it is
- Tells you in no uncertain terms
- Tells you like it or lump it
- Tells you no ifs, ands or buts
- Tells you straight from the shoulder
- Tells you the bitter truth
- Tells you up front

## OR CAN BE DESCRIBED AS:

- A man of few words

# THE SMOOTH TALKER

## THE SMOOTH TALKER IS A:

Con Man, Glib Talker, Pitch Man, Sweet-Talker.

## AND CAN BE CHARACTERIZED BY THE FOLLOWING:

- Butter would melt in his mouth
- Carefully crafts his words
- Chooses his words carefully
- Could sell air conditioners in Alaska
- Eases into what he has to say
- Easy on the ears—controls his speech
- Examines every word before he says it

- Gives you a song and dance
- Honey drips from his tongue
- Lulls you into a sense of security
- Plays with words
- Pussyfoots around in getting to the point
- Puts a spin on his words
- Slips in his point unnoticed
- Slips it to you smoothly
- Soft-soaps you
- Speaks politically correct
- Sugarcoats his words
- Talks in a silky voice
- Talks tongue in cheek
- Tells you what you want to hear
- Tones down his criticisms
- Uses child psychology on you
- Uses double meanings
- Uses flowery speech
- Uses polite language
- Uses the King's English
- Watches his mouth
- Waters down his comments

## OR CAN BE DESCRIBED AS:

- A soap-box orator

# THE DISQUIETING TALKER

## THE DISQUIETING TALKER IS A:

Complainer, Double-Talker, Loud Mouth, Screamer, Whiner, Yeller.

## AND CAN BE CHARACTERIZED BY THE FOLLOWING:

- Barks at you
- Beats around the bush
- Bitches
- Blows his own horn
- Blows hot air
- Blows smoke
- Cuts you to the quick
- Drags out a story
- Garbles his speech
- Gets into shouting matches
- Gets tongue-tied
- Gives you a snow job
- Grates on your nerves
- Has a sharp tongue
- Has a vicious tongue
- Makes cutting remarks
- Murders the King's English
- Shoots from the hip
- Shouts you down
- Sounds off
- Speaks gobbledy-gook
- Speaks Pigeon English

- Speaks with a forked tongue
- Speaks with his mouth full
- Spouts profanities
- Steps on his own tongue
- Stutters and stammers
- Takes forever to say it
- Talks a good fight
- Talks crap
- Talks dirty
- Talks down to people
- Talks in circles
- Talks like he has a mouth full of marbles
- Talks nonsense
- Talks over everyone else
- Talks over one's head
- Talks psychobabble
- Talks street talk
- Talks through his hat
- Talks you deaf, dumb and blind
- Talks out of both sides of his mouth
- Tells cock-and-bull stories
- Throws the bull
- Uses abrasive speech
- Uses gutter talk
- Uses rough language
- Uses weasel-words
- You can't believe a word he says

## OR CAN BE DESCRIBED AS:

- One who abuses his speaking privileges

# MEANINGFUL CONVERSATION

## MEANINGFUL CONVERSATION IS A:

Brain Session, Business Talk, Conference, Friendly Discussion, Heart-To-Heart Talk, Polite Conversation, Powwow, Private Discussion.

## AND CAN BE CHARACTERIZED BY THE FOLLOWING:

- Bandy words
- Expressing your honest opinion
- Getting down to brass tacks
- Having words with someone
- Kicking ideas around
- Professional
- Reasoning with someone
- Sincere speech
- Speaking your mind
- Stating your feelings
- Talking over a problem
- Talking pleasantly to someone
- Talking sense

- Talking things out
- Talking to one like a Dutch uncle

- Discussing matters intelligently

## OR CAN BE DESCRIBED AS:

- Exchanging points of view

# LESS THAN FORTHRIGHT

## TO BE LESS THAN FORTHRIGHT IS TO BE:

Blowing Smoke, Blowing Up A Story, Bluffing, Conning Someone, Covering Up, Creating A False Impression, Distorting The Facts, Expanding The Facts, Giving Someone A Snow-Job, Hiding The Truth, Hood-Winking Someone, Misstating The Facts, Playing Loose With The Facts, Playing With Words, Pulling The Wool Over Someone's Eyes, Skating Over The Truth, Skirting The Truth, Straying From The Truth, Talking Double-Talk, Telling A Half-Truth, Telling Half A Story, Trampling The Truth, Twisting The Truth, Using Weasel Words.

## AND CAN BE CHARACTERIZED BY THE FOLLOWING:

- Avoiding the issue
- Believes "What he doesn't know won't hurt him"
- Building up a story
- Challenging one's sense of the credible
- Clouding the issue
- Concocting a story
- Conjuring up an alibi
- Cooking up an excuse
- Dreaming up an alibi
- Feeding one a line
- Fudging the facts

- Giving a cozy answer
- Giving one a song and a dance
- Glossing over the facts
- Going around the bam with an explanation
- Hedging on an explanation
- Hemming and hawing
- Hiding behind an omission
- Insulting someone's intelligence
- Inventing an explanation
- Making a sales pitch
- Manufacturing an alibi

- Not coming clean
- Omitting pertinent details
- Omitting some small details
- Palming off an explanation
- Putting a spin on a story
- Selling one a bill of goods
- Skimping on the facts
- Skipping details
- Soft-soaping someone
- Speaking tongue-in-cheek
- Speaking with a forked tongue
- Spinning a yarn
- Stone-walling
- Sugarcoating the story
- Sweet-talking someone
- Talking around a subject
- Talking clap-trap
- Talking gibberish
- Talking gobbledy-gook
- Talking in circles
- Talking lawyer-talk
- Talking legalese
- Talking nonsense
- Talking out of both sides of your mouth
- Talking psycho-babble
- Talking through your hat
- Tap-dancing around a fact
- Telling a wild story
- Telling stories
- Testing someone's gullibility
- Understating a problem
- Waltzing around a subject

## OR CAN BE DESCRIBED AS:

- Being glib
- Being less than candid
- Bending the truth
- Concealing the truth
- Embellishing the truth
- Stretching the truth

# LIES LIES AND MORE LIES

## TO LIE IS TO:

Bullshit Someone, Deceive Someone, Dump A Load Of Bull On One, Exaggerate The Truth, Fabricate A Story, Fail To Mention A Detail, Fiddle With The Facts, Give A False Version Of The Facts, Give One A Lot Of Baloney, Give Someone A Bunch Of Crap, Give Someone A Line, Give Someone Blarney, Gussy Up A Story, Jive Someone, Leave Out Part Of The Story, Make A False Statement, Peddle Manure, Pile It High And Deep, Pull Someone's Leg, Shovel The Crap, Snooker Someone, Tell A Fib, Tell A Whopper, Tell Tall Tales, Throw The Bull, Twist The Truth All Out Of Shape, Use Double Meanings.

## AND CAN BE CHARACTERIZED BY THE FOLLOWING:

- A practiced liar
- An experienced liar
- An unabashed liar
- Believes his own lies
- Can't believe a word he says
- Departing from the facts
- Dressing up the facts
- Giving one a lot of garbage
- Giving one the soft-sell
- He lies to hear himself talking
- He wouldn't recognize the truth if it stared him in the face
- Inflating a report Insulting one's intelligence
- Leading one to believe a lie
- Look one in the face and lie
- Lying as a second nature
- Lying for the sake of lying
- Lying in your teeth
- Lying like a rug
- Lying out of habit
- Lying to cover a lie
- Lying to someone's face
- Lying with a straight face
- Making it up as you go along
- Overlooking a few facts
- Padding your resume
- Playing hob with the truth
- Playing on one's naivete
- Playing one for a fool
- Playing one for a sucker
- Poppycock!
- Puffing up an account
- Putting up a false front
- Selling one a bill of goods
- Selling one the Brooklyn Bridge
- Soft-selling someone
- Stringing someone along
- Taking advantage of someone's gullibility
- Taking it with a grain of salt
- Talking gibberish
- Telling a cock-and-bull story
- Telling a fish story
- Telling a little white lie
- Telling a pack of lies
- Telling a story bordering on the ridiculous
- Telling bald-faced lies
- Telling bare-faced lies
- Tommy-rot!
- What he doesn't know won't hurt him
- Whipping up an excuse

## OR CAN BE DESCRIBED AS:

- Abusing the truth
- Being a pathological liar
- Being careless with the truth
- Concealing the truth
- Playing fast and loose with the facts
- Playing with the truth
- Taking liberties with the truth
- Weaving a web of deceit

# WORDS OF ROMANCE

**WORDS OF ROMANCE ARE:**

Cupid's Arrows, Hot Words, Smoldering Words, Terms Of Endearment, Words Of Love.

**AND CAN BE CHARACTERIZED BY THE FOLLOWING:**

- Being attracted to someone
- Blind date
- Boy friend
- Bussing someone
- Carry the torch for someone
- Coming on to someone
- Dating
- Fooling around
- Getting to first base
- Getting turned on by someone
- Girl friend
- Giving one lip service
- Giving someone a line
- Giving someone a second look
- Giving someone the eye
- Going all the way
- Going out with someone
- Going steady
- Hanging out
- Having a crush on someone
- Having a roll in the hay
- Having a thing for someone
- Having the hots for someone
- Heavy date
- Hop in the sack with someone
- Leering at someone
- Living in
- Making a date with someone
- Making a move on someone
- Making a pass at someone
- Making love
- Making out
- Making time with someone
- Making up to someone
- Meaningful relationship
- Moving in on someone
- Ogling someone
- On the make
- On the prowl
- Picking someone up
- Playing around on someone
- Playing games with someone
- Playing hard to get
- Playing it cool
- Playing the field
- Scoring
- Serious date
- Shacking up
- Significant other
- Sleeping with someone

- Smooching
- Swapping spit

- Wearing your heart on your sleeve

## AND CAN BE CHARACTERIZED AS

- The language of Venus

# XIV
# THINKING POWER

# BRAINY PEOPLE

## BRAINY PEOPLE ARE:

Book-Worms, Brain Surgeons, Bright People, Brilliant People, Clever Cookies, Eggheads, Geniuses, Gurus, Know-It-Alls, Quick Studies, Rocket Scientists, Sharpies, Smart Alecks, Smart-Asses, Smart-Mouths, Smartie-Pants, Whiz Kids, Whizzes, Wise Apples, Wise Guys, Wisenheimers.

## AND CAN BE CHARACTERIZED BY THE FOLLOWING:

- Has his wits about him
- Has it all together
- In the know
- Knows his way around
- Knows which end is up
- No flies on him
- No moss growing on him
- No slouch
- Nobody's fool
- Not behind the door when the smarts were handed out
- On top of things
- Someone to be proud of
- Too smart for his own good

## OR CAN BE DESCRIBED AS:

- Brilliant
- Keen as a razor
- Keen-minded
- Quick on his feet
- Razor sharp
- Sharp as a tack
- Smart as a whip
- Wise as an owl

# UNDERSTAND/COMPREHEND

## TO UNDERSTAND/COMPREHEND IS TO:

Catch On, Dig It, Fathom It, Get A Rash, Get A Hold On It, Get The Point, Get Wise, Have A Bulb Light Up, Have It Add Up For You, Have It Click, Have It Come Out Of The Blue, Have It Dawn On You, Have It Hit You, Have It Pop In Your Head, Have It Register, Savvy It, See It, See The Light.

## AND CAN BE CHARACTERIZED BY THE FOLLOWING:

- Adding two and two together
- Coming alive
- Coming to grips with it
- Coming to realize it
- Coming up with the answer
- Eureka!
- Figuring it out Getting a grip
- Getting clued in Getting hep
- Getting hit over the head with it
- Getting it straight
- Getting the swing of it
- Getting with it
- Grabbing onto itHaving it made clear to you
- Having it sneak up on you
- Making sense of it
- Opening your eyes to it
- Putting the pieces together
- Reasoning it out
- Smartening up
- Solving it
- Waking up to the facts
- Wising up
- Working your way through it
- Zeroing in on it

## OR CAN BE DESCRIBED AS:

- Catching the drift Getting it through your head

# HAVING DIFFICULTY SOLVING A PROBLEM

## TO HAVE DIFFICULTY SOLVING A PROBLEM IS TO BE:

All At Sea, Bamboozled, Buffaloed, Bumbling Around, Floundering Around, Flying Blind, Going Around In Circles, Going Bananas, Going Bonkers, Groping In The Dark, In A Dilemma, In A Maze, In A Rut, In An Alien World, Knocking Your Head Against The Wall, Lost In A Fog, Lost In The Woods, Mired Down, Rattling Your Brains, Running Into Roadblocks, Sailing Without A Rudder, Spinning Your Wheels, Stuck In The Mud, Stumbling Around In The Dark, Stumbling Over Your Own Feet, Stumped, Up A Blind Alley, Up The Creek Without A Paddle.

## AND CAN BE CHARACTERIZED BY THE FOLLOWING:

- Back where you started
- Beating your brains out
- Booting the ball around
- Bumping into walls

- Can't get off the ground
- Can't get there from here
- Can't make heads or tails of it
- Can't make sense out of it
- Can't put the pieces together
- Can't see the forest for the trees
- Coming to a grinding halt
- Doesn't have a glimmer
- Doesn't know which end is up
- Going from bad to worse
- Haven't a clue
- Haven't got the foggiest
- Having blinders on
- It's all Greek to me
- It s all over my head
- Lost all direction
- Meeting yourself coming and going
- Not within striking distance
- Out of ideas
- Retracing your steps over a barrel
- Running around like a chicken with its head cut off
- Striking out in all directions
- Suffering from a temporary case of amnesia

## OR CAN BE DESCRIBED AS:

- Adrift in a sea of confusion
- Being utterly confused
- Getting bogged down
- Getting stymied

# WAYS OF IMPARTING KNOWLEDGE

## TO IMPART KNOWLEDGE IS TO:

Break The News, Bring One Up To Date, Clue Someone In, Drive The Point Across, Fill Someone In, Give One An Earful, Give Someone A Friendly Tip, Give Someone The Dope, Give Someone The Lowdown, Give Someone The Poop, Give Someone The Scoop, Give Someone The Skinny, Give Someone The Word, Lay It On Someone, Lay It On The Line, Lay It Out For Someone, Let Someone In On It, Let Someone Know What's Up, Mince No Words, Talk To One Like A Dutch Uncle, Talk Turkey, Teach Someone A Thing Or Two, Teach Someone The Ropes, Tell It Like It Is, Tell Someone What's Coming Down, Tip Someone Off.

## AND CAN BE CHARACTERIZED BY THE FOLLOWING:

- Alerting one to the facts
- Banging someone's ears
- Beating around the bush about it

- Bringing it home to someone
- Clearing up one's doubts
- Dragging someone into the twentieth century
- Dumping it on someone
- Easing into it
- Feeding it to one slowly
- Force feeding someone
- Giving it to someone straight
- Giving one the G-2
- Giving one the sordid details
- Giving someone the bad news
- Giving someone the facts of life
- Giving someone the whole story
- Hinting at it
- Hitting one between the eyes with it
- Hitting one in the gut with it
- Hitting one over the head with it
- Leading up to it slowly
- Leaving no doubt in his mind
- Making it known to him
- Making no bones about it
- Making one aware of the facts
- Making one privy to the facts
- Making one see the light
- Making one sit up and listen
- Making someone swallow it
- Opening one's eyes
- Pulling no punches
- Ramming it down someone's throat
- Saying it over and over
- Shaking someone up
- Sitting him down and talking to him
- Slapping someone in the face with it
- Slipping it to one gently
- Spelling it out for someone
- Spoon-feeding someone
- Sugarcoating it
- Taking one into your confidence
- Telling one in no uncertain terms
- Telling one like you mean it
- Telling one no ifs, ands or buts
- Telling one outright
- Telling one straight from the shoulder
- Telling one the bitter truth
- Waking someone up to the facts
- Wasting no words telling one

## OR CAN BE DESCRIBED AS:

- Bringing it out in the open
- Drumming it in to someone
- Getting it across to someone
- Knocking some sense into someone
- Running it by someone
- Straightening someone out
- Wising someone up

# THE THOUGHT PROCESS

## TO THINK IS TO:

Brainstorm, Cogitate On It, Concentrate On Something, Consider The Pros And Cons, Digest It, Kick It Around In Your Head, Meditate On It, Mull It Over, Noodle It, Ponder It, Wrack Your Brain.

## AND CAN BE CHARACTERIZED BY THE FOLLOWING:

- Dwelling on it
- Giving it some sink time
- Letting it simmer
- Letting it sink in
- Massaging it
- Putting it under a microscope
- Putting your thinking cap on
- Sleeping on it
- Thinking it through
- Wrestling with it

## OR CAN BE DESCRIBED AS:

- Chewing on it
- Turning it over in your head
- Using some brain power
- Working it over in your brain

# CAUTIOUS

## TO BE CAUTIOUS IS TO:

Be Sure Of Your Ground, Beware Of Greeks Bringing Gifts, Have Eyes In The Back Of Your Head, Hear No Evil—See No Evil—Speak No Evil, Keep A Weather Eye Out, Keep Your Eyes Peeled And Your Ears Open, Look Before You Leap, Mind Your Own Business, Monitor Your Speech, Put A Finger In The Wind, Put A Rein On Your Tongue, Put A Toe In The Water, Send Up A Trial Balloon, Zipper Your Mouth.

## AND CAN BE CHARACTERIZED BY THE FOLLOWING:

- Accepting the status quo
- Don't be lulled into a sense of false security
- Don't bite off more than you can chew
- Don't bite off your nose to spite your face
- Don't buck the tide
- Don't lock the bam after the horse is gone
- Don't look for trouble
- Don't open a can of worms
- Don't open Pandora's box
- Don't poke a hornet's nest
- Don't rock the boat
- Don't stir the ashes
- Don't wake a sleeping giant
- Going along for the ride
- Half a loaf is better than none
- If it ain't broke, don't fix it
- Knowing which way the wind blows
- Leaving well enough alone
- Letting sleeping dogs lie
- Looking both ways before stepping off the curb
- Rolling with the punches
- Settling out of court
- Taking nothing for granted
- Turning the other cheek

## OR CAN BE DESCRIBED AS:

- Keeping your powder dry
- Watching your step

# GIVE IT SOME THOUGHT

## TO GIVE IT SOME THOUGHT IS TO:

Analyze It, Brainstorm It, Chew On It, Concentrate On It, Digest It, Keep It On The Front Burner, Mull It Over, Noodle It, Ponder It, Sleep On It, Study It, Weigh It Carefully, Wrestle With It.

## AND CAN BE CHARACTERIZED BY THE FOLLOWING:

- Dwelling on it
- Giving it time to settle in
- Letting it gel
- Letting it simmer
- Letting it sink in
- Putting it under the microscope
- Thinking of it every which way

## OR CAN BE DESCRIBED AS:

- Kicking it around in your head
- Scratching your head on it

- Turning it over in your head
- Working it over in your brain

# NOT VERY BRIGHT

## ONE WHO IS NOT A ROCKET SCIENTIST IS A:

Birdbrain, Boob, Bumbler, Clobber-Head, Clod, Clown, Crackpot, Deadhead, Dipsy, Doofus, Dum-Dum, Dumbbell, Dunderhead, Dweeb, Fathead, Feather-Brain, Fool, Geek, Goof-Ball, Goofus, Hare-Brain, Jerk, Know-Nothing, Knuck-lehead, Kook, Lame-Brain, Loser, Lunkhead, Nerd, Nincompoop, Nitwit, Nobody, Numbskull, Pea Brain, Peanut Brain, Simpleton, Twerp, Wacko, Zero.

## AND CAN BE CHARACTERIZED BY THE FOLLOWING:

- Bumping into walls
- Can't add two and two
- Can't find his way home
- Can't put one foot past the other without tripping
- Can't see past his nose
- Can't tell his butt from a hole in the ground
- Couldn't find something if it rose up and bit him
- Doesn't have the sense he was bom with
- Doesn't know diddly squat Doesn't know enough to come in out of the rain
- Doesn't know which end is up
- Flew over his head
- Forgets his own name
- Gets lost in a phone booth

- Has a head that comes to a point
- Has a hole in his head
- Has a screw loose
- Has a sieve for a brain
- Has bats in the belfry
- Has only one oar in the water
- Has rocks in his head
- Has to be led around by the hand
- Hasn't got the foggiest
- His bus left
- Is one brick shy of a load
- Lights are on but nobody's home
- Lost his marbles
- Lost in a fog
- Mush for brains
- Nobody home upstairs

- Nothing between his ears
- Nutty as a fruitcake
- Someone rang his bell
- Trips over his own feet
- Walking around in a fog
- Walks around wearing blinders
- Wanders around in a daze
- Was behind the door when the smarts were handed out
- When it comes to brains he got the short end of the stick
- Would lose his head if it wasn't fastened to his neck
- Wouldn't see something until it slapped him in the face

## OR CAN BE DESCRIBED AS:

- Addle-headed
- An airhead
- An idiot
- Batty
- Bonkers
- Brainless
- Cracked
- Crazy as a loon
- Dopey
- Dumb as a stone
- Dumb as an ox
- Empty-headed
- Forgetful
- Hollow-headed
- Hopeless
- Nuts
- Nutty
- Off the wall
- Out of it
- Scatter-brained
- Simple-minded
- Slap-happy

# ABSOLUTE/FINAL JUDGMENT

## AN ABSOLUTE/FINAL JUDGMENT IS A:

Clear-Cut Case, Closed Case, Cut And Dried Decision, Final Answer, Foregone Conclusion, Shoo-In.

## AND CAN BE CHARACTERIZED BY THE FOLLOWING:

- A sure thing
- Absolute pits
- As bad as it gets
- As certain as death and taxes
- As sure as I am of my own name
- As sure as I'm standing here
- Beyond the shadow of a doubt

- Couldn't be clearer
- Dead as a doornail
- For absolute certain
- Hit rock bottom
- I'll bet a week's wages on it
- I'll stake my life on it
- It couldn't be better
- It's a closed book
- It's a done deal
- It's a waste of your breath talking about it
- It's as final as death
- It's over and done
- It's water over the dam
- It's water under the bridge
- Like it or lump it
- My mind is totally made up
- Never more sure of anything in my life
- No conceivable alternative
- No doubt about it
- No getting away from it
- No ifs, ands or buts
- No sense crying over spilled milk
- No sense talking about it further
- No turning back No other way
- No sense in beating a dead horse
- No way around it

- Not a glimmer of hope
- Not a snowball's chance in hell
- Not the faintest hope left
- Plain as day
- Plain as the nose on your face
- Positively the last straw
- Sink or swim
- Sure as God made little green apples
- Sure as shootin'
- Sure as sin
- The die is cast
- The point of no return
- What's done is done
- What you see is what you get
- Without question
- Without the slightest question
- Worst case condition
- Wrong as sin
- You can make a book on it
- You can't get blood out of a turnip
- You can't get water out of a stone
- You don't have a leg to stand on
- You don't have a prayer
- You have to live with it
- You made your bed, now lie in it
- You're finished!

## OR CAN BE DESCRIBED AS:

- As final as Omega
- As irreversible as death

- Beyond dispute
- Right as rain

# XV
# TIME

# CONSIDERING TIME

**TIME IS A:**

Century, Decade, Definite Portion Of Duration, Hour, Measurement Of Our Days, Millenium, Millisecond, Minute, Moment, Nanosecond, Period, Season, Second, Year.

**AND CAN BE CHARACTERIZED BY THE FOLLOWING:**

- Any time you say
- At any time
- Doing time
- Fun time
- Having a hard time
- Having a hot time
- Having the time of your life
- In due time
- In the nick of time
- In time
- In your own sweet time
- Just in time
- Killing time
- Losing time
- Making time for someone
- Making time with someone
- No time like the present
- Oftentimes On time
- On your own time
- Out of time
- Over time Saving time
- Sometimes
- Spend time with someone
- Telling time
- The end of time
- The time has passed for it
- The time will come for it
- There's a time for everything
- Time-and-a-half
- Time and tide wait for no man
- Time and time again
- Time is against you
- Time is catching up with you
- Time is up!
- Time it
- Time it right
- Time left over
- Time of day
- Time of night Time off
- Time on your hands
- Time on your side
- Time out
- Time stands still
- Time-tested
- Time to go
- Time to kill
- Time to spare
- Time was when we could
- Time will tell
- Timeworn
- Times to come
- Times to remember
- When the time is right

## OR CAN BE DESCRIBED AS:

- Bad
- Borrowed
- Correct
- Dragging
- Easy
- Fast
- Fleeting
- Flying
- Found
- Free
- Good
- Happy
- Hard
- Idle
- Lost
- Passing
- Past
- Quick
- Right
- Sad
- Short
- Slow
- Still
- Terrible
- Wasted
- Well-spent
- Writing

# TO WAIT ANXIOUSLY

## WAITING IS:

Biding your time, Hanging Around, Holding Your Horses, Killing Time, Left Suspended, Pending The Outcome, Sweating It Out.

## AND CAN BE CHARACTERIZED BY THE FOLLOWING:

- Biting your fingernails
- Chomping at the bit
- Cooling your heels
- Drumming your fingers
- Getting antsy
- Getting anxious
- Having your mouth watering
- Holding your breath
- Holding your water
- Keeping occupied
- Left hanging
- On the alert
- Pacing the floor
- Pawing the ground
- Playing the waiting game
- Queuing up
- Running out of patience
- Shifting from one foot to the other
- Sitting in traffic

- Sitting on pins and needles
- Sitting on the edge of the seat
- Straining at the leash
- Tapping your feet
- Twiddling your thumbs
- Wait for me!
- Wait for the right time to do it
- Wait 'til I get my hands on you!
- Wait until your father comes home!
- Wait your chance
- Wait your turn at bat
- Waiting an eternity
- Waiting for the bell
- Waiting for the other shoe to drop
- Waiting for your ship to come in
- Waiting in line
- Waiting in the wings
- Waiting in vain
- Waiting on one hand and foot
- Waiting on someone
- Waiting someone out
- Waiting up for someone
- Waiting your turn
- Watch and wait

## OR CAN BE DESCRIBED AS

- Being patient and impatient
- Counting the minutes
- Watching the clock

# CLOSE

## CLOSE IS:

A Step Away, A Stone's Throw Away, Around The Corner, Around The Next Turn, At Your Fingertips, Just Over The Hill, Up The Road A Piece, Within Sight, Within Your Grasp.

## AND CAN BE CHARACTERIZED BY THE FOLLOWING:

- At your beck and call
- Beckoning to you
- Close at hand
- Close to death
- Close to home
- Close to tears
- Close to the edge
- Close to the end
- Close to your heart
- Get a close shave
- Have a close call
- Have a close friend

- Have a close shave
- Make a close call
- You can reach out and touch it

## OR CAN BE DESCRIBED AS:

- Not far away
- Not far in the future

# VERY CLOSE

## VERY CLOSE IS:

A Heartbeat Away, Hanging By A Thread, On The Cutting Edge, On The Edge, Skating On Thin Ice, Skin-Tight, Skirting The Edge, Standing On The Ledge, Staring Death In The Face.

## AND CAN BE CHARACTERIZED BY THE FOLLOWING:

- About to explode
- Beat within an inch of your life
- Having someone breathing down your neck
- Holding your breath
- Just by the hair on your chin
- Knowing "There but for the grace of God go I"
- Looking into the jaws of death
- Made it by a hair's breadth
- Missed by a cat's whisker
- Missed by an eyelash
- Missed by an inch
- Off by a gnat's lash
- On the brink of disaster
- On the verge of tears
- Ready to pop
- Saved by the bell
- Saved by the skin of your teeth
- Waiting with bated breath

## OR CAN BE DESCRIBED AS:

- Being right under your nose
- Having the narrowest of margins

# QUICK

**QUICK IS:**

All Of A Sudden, At A Moment's Notice, At The Drop Of A Hat, In A Heartbeat, In A Jiffy, In The Bat Of An Eye, In The Blink Of An Eye, In The Snap Of A Finger.

**AND CAN BE CHARACTERIZED BY THE FOLLOWING:**

- Before I could catch my breath
- Before I could open my mouth
- Before I knew what hit me
- Before you could blink
- Before you could say Jack Robinson
- Before you could think
- Before you could turn around
- Before you knew it
- Quick as a flash
- Quick as a wink
- Without hesitation
- Without thinking
- Without warning

**OR CAN BE DESCRIBED AS:**

- As fast as greased lightning
- As fast as lightning
- As quick as a bunny

# LASTS A LONG TIME

**LASTS A LONG TIME IS:**

Forever And A Day, On And On , Ad Infinitum, Perpetual Motions, Sequels, Without End, Year In And Year Out.

## AND CAN BE CHARACTERIZED BY THE FOLLOWING:

- As lasting as a mother's love
- As long as it takes
- Built to last
- Continuing without interruption
- For as long as I live
- For the foreseeable future
- I will carry it to my grave
- Improves with time
- Into the indefinite future
- Lifetime guarantee
- No end in sight
- Open-end agreement
- Over and over again
- Over the long haul
- 'Til death do us part
- Until hell freezes over
- Until my dying day
- Until the cows come home
- Until the sun sets in the East
- Will outlive you and me
- While I live and breathe
- While there's a breath left in me

## OR CAN BE DESCRIBED AS:

- As enduring as life itself
- From a to z
- From Alpha to Omega
- From here on out
- From here to eternity
- From now on
- From start to finish
- From the beginning to the end
- From the cradle to the grave

# FINAL FINISHES

## FINAL FINISHES ARE:

Closing Chapters, Done Deals, Final Agreements, Final Blows, Final Bow, Final Conclusions, Final Moments, Grand Finales, Last Chances, Last Farewells, Last Gasps, Last Hurrahs, Last Words, Wipeouts.

## AND CAN BE CHARACTERIZED BY THE FOLLOWING:

- After all is said and done
- All wrapped up
- At a dead end
- At the end of your rope
- At your wits' end
- Coming down to the wire
- Crossed the finish line
- Dead to the world

- Down to the wire
- Dying breath
- Gone and forgotten
- It's over and done
- Last but not least
- Out of gas
- Over the hill
- Pooped
- Rock-bottom prices
- Shot your load
- Swinging at the end of a rope
- The bottom line
- The bottom of the barrel
- The end of the line
- The end of the road
- The last straw
- Thrown on the junk heap
- Water over the dam
- When the fat lady sings
- When time has run out

**OR CAN BE DESCRIBED AS:**

- Last ditch efforts

# REMAIN

**WHEN YOU REMAIN, YOU:**

Claim Squatter's Rights, Drop Anchor, Hang Up Your Hat, Hole Up, Hunker Down, Move In, Pitch Your Tent, Plunk Yourself Down, Put Down Your Roots, Stake A Claim, Stay Put, Stick Around, Take Up Quarters, Take Up Residence, Unpack Your Bags.

**AND CAN BE CHARACTERIZED BY THE FOLLOWING:**

- Digging in
- Finding a home
- Have a key made
- In for the night
- Making yourself at home
- Making yourself cozy
- Moving in for keeps
- Moving in with your trunk
- Overstaying your welcome
- Putting your shoes under the bed
- Taking over the premises
- Taking up light housekeeping

**OR CAN BE DESCRIBED AS:**

- Hanging around
- Hanging on

# GIVING SOMEONE GREATER INDEPENDENCE

## WHEN YOU GIVE SOMEONE GREATER INDEPENDENCE, YOU:

Break His Chains, Cut His Bonds, Ease Up On Him, Free Him Up, Get Off His Back, Give Him Free Rein, Give Him Freedom Of Choice, Give Him Greater Latitude, Give Him His Head, Give Him Some Slack, Let Down The Bars, Let Up On His Reins, Loosen Your Grip On Him, Open The Gates For Him, Relax Your Hold On Him, Remove Your Constraints, Set Him Free, Turn Him Loose, Unbridle Him, Uncuff Him, Unfetter Him, Unshackle Him, Untie The Apron Strings.

## AND CAN BE CHARACTERIZED BY THE FOLLOWING:

- Letting him off the hook
- Letting him out from under
- Letting him run loose
- Lightening his load
- Lowering the barriers
- Removing obstacles in his path

## OR CAN BE DESCRIBED AS:

- Emancipating someone
- Giving him a better shake
- Giving him his freedom
- Giving him his own key
- Leaving him on his own
- Leaving him to his own devices
- Letting him fend for himself
- Letting him find his own way
- Letting him go off on his own
- Letting him make his own decisions

# POSSIBILITIES

## WHEN THERE IS A POSSIBILITY:

It All Depends, It Can Go Either Way, It Could Happen, It Depends On How The Ball Bounces, It Depends On How The Cards Fall, It Depends On How The Cookie Crumbles, It Depends On The Fickle Finger Of Fate, It's A Crap

Shoot, It's A Long Shot, It's A Throw Of The Dice, It's Anyone's Guess, It's A Spin On The Wheel, It's Got A Shot, It's Worth A Shot, It's Up To The Gods, There's A Chance, There's No Telling, There's No Way Of Knowing.

## AND CAN BE CHARACTERIZED BY THE FOLLOWING:

- Chances are
- Could be
- Hopefully
- If Dame Fortune smiles on you
- If everything falls right
- If it all comes together
- If it's in the cards
- If Lady Luck is with you
- If the pieces fit
- If you play your cards right
- If you're lucky
- It's not over until the fat lady sings
- Maybe
- Never say "die!"
- Perhaps
- Sit tight and hope
- Somebody has to win
- There's an outside chance
- This may be your lucky day
- We'll have to wait and see
- What have you got to lose
- When you least expect it
- With a little bit of luck
- You never know!

## OR CAN BE DESCRIBED AS:

- Not being dead in the water yet

# XVI
# TROUBLE, TURMOIL
# AND COMMOTION

# PHYSICAL DISPUTE

## A PHYSICAL DISPUTE IS A:

Brawl, Donnybrook, Free-For-All, Hand-To-Hand Scuffle, Knock-Down/Drag-Out, Melee, No-Holds-Barred Battle, Punch Party, Rumble, Scrap, Slug-Fest.

## AND CAN BE CHARACTERIZED BY THE FOLLOWING:

- Bashing heads
- Beating someone black and blue
- Beating someone senseless
  Beating someone soundly
- Beating someone to a fare-thee-well
- Beating someone to a pulp
- Beating someone within an inch of his life
- Beating someone's brains out
- Beating the tar out of someone
- Blacking someone's eyes
- Bloodying someone's nose
- Boxing someone's ears
- Breaking every bone in someone's body
- Clobbering someone
- Cold-cocking someone
- Creaming someone
- Crowning someone
- Decking someone
- Downing someone
- Driving someone into the ground
- Flailing out in all directions
- Flattening someone
- Flooring someone
- Getting in a barroom brawl
- Getting in the ring with someone
- Giving someone a boxing lesson
- Giving someone a fat lip
- Giving someone a knuckle sandwich
- Hitting him with everything but the kitchen sink
- Hitting one up side of the head
- K.O. someone
- Kicking butts
- Kicking the tar out of someone
- Knocking someone into next Sunday
- Knocking someone around
- Knock someone cold
- Knocking someone from pillar to post
- Knocking someone into Kingdom come
- Knocking someone unconscious

- Knocking someone's head off
- Knocking someone's teeth out
- Knocking the daylights out of someone
- Knocking the stuffing out of someone
- Laying into someone
- Laying someone out
- Laying someone up for a week
- Licking someone soundly
- Lowering the boom on someone
- Pasting someone
- Plastering someone
- Pounding someone silly
- Punching someone's lights out
- Putting on the gloves
- Putting someone down for the count
- Sending someone sprawling
- Slapping someone silly
- Slugging someone
- Smashing someone
- Socking someone
- Splitting someone's lip
- Spreading someone's nose all over his face
- Stomping on someone
- Sucker punching someone
- Swatting someone
- Swinging at anything that moves
- Taking someone apart piece by piece
- The manly art of self-defense
- Throwing leather at someone
- Throwing your Sunday punch
- Trading blows with someone
- Trouncing someone
- Walloping someone
- Whacking someone
- Whipping someone's ass

## OR CAN BE DESCRIBED AS:

- Engaging in fisticuffs
- Giving someone his lumps
- Going at it with someone
- Going to the mat with someone
- Going toe-to-toe with someone
- Mixing it up with someone
- Putting up your dukes with one
- Squaring off with someone
- Taking someone on

# AVOID CONFRONTATION

## TO AVOID CONFRONTATION IS TO:

Act Civilized, Back Off A Little, Bite Your Lip, Bite Your Tongue, Bury The Hatchet, Control Your Temper, Count To Ten, Duck The Issue, Exercise

Restraint, Hide Your Feelings, Hold Your Horses, Hold Your Water, Ignore A Comment, Keep A Leash On Your Tongue, Keep A Lid On Your Emotions, Keep A Poker Face, Keep A Rein On Your Anger, Keep Your Voice Down, Kiss And Make Up, Parry A Comment, Shake Hands And Make Up, Sidestep The Issue, Sidetrack The Issue, Smoke The Peace Pipe, Speak Softly, Stifle An Urge To Fight Back, Turn The Other Cheek, Walk Away From It, Watch Your Mouth, Zipper Your Lip.

## AND CAN BE CHARACTERIZED BY THE FOLLOWING:

- Cutting someone some slack
- Disdaining the use of force
- Don't add fuel to the fire
- Don't be a judge and jury
- Don't examine his every word
- Don't get ruffled
- Don't let it cloud your judgment
- Don't let it faze you
- Don't make a mountain out of a molehill
- Don't make waves
- Don't rock the boat
- Easing into a situation
- Giving a little, taking a little
- Giving someone a fair shake
- Giving someone an ear
- Giving someone his turn at bat
- Giving someone simple justice
- Gritting your teeth
- Letting a remark pass
- Letting him have his say
- Letting it run off you like water off a duck
- Letting him have his day in court
- Letting him speak his piece
- Letting him spout his venom
- Letting someone have his fifteen minutes in the sun
- Listening with both ears
- Looking at both sides of the coin
- Looking at it through someone else's eyes
- Looking for the good in someone
- Offering someone common courtesy
- Playing for time
- Pulling in your horns
- Pulling your punches
- Putting the shoe on the other foot
- Putting yourself in someone else's place
- Seeking common ground
- Soft-peddling an issue
- Splitting the difference
- Standing in their shoes for a moment
- Taking things in stride
- Taking time to cool off
- Taking what he says with a grain of salt
- Using a soft-sell
- Walking in someone else's footsteps

**OR CAN BE DESCRIBED AS:**

- Being calm, cool and collected
- Being laid-back

- Playing it cool
- Playing it low-key

## ASKING FOR TROUBLE

**ASKING FOR TROUBLE IS:**

Carrying A Chip On Your Shoulder, Cruising For A Bruising, Daring The Devil, Defying Common Sense, Flirting With Danger, Getting On People's Nerves, Getting Out Of Bounds, Getting Out Of Line, Getting Up In Someone's Face, Making A Nuisance Of Yourself, Mouthing Off At People, Opening A Can Of Worms, Opening Pandora's Box, Picking A Fight, Playing With Fire, Pushing Your Luck, Putting Your Neck In A Noose, Scoffing At The Law, Shooting Off Your Mouth, Skating On Thin Ice, Skirting The Edge, Stepping On People's Toes, Sticking Your Nose In Where It Doesn't Belong, Stirring Up Trouble, Tempting Fate, Throwing Caution To The Wind, Throwing Down The Gauntlet, Thumbing Your Nose At Authority, Walking A Tightrope.

**AND CAN BE CHARACTERIZED BY THE FOLLOWING:**

- Acting like a jackass
- Adding fuel to the fire
- Backstabbing
- Burning your bridges behind you
- Butting into other people's business
- Causing everyone's patience to wear thin
- Challenging the odds
- Coming on strong
- Crossing the line
- Flying in the face of danger
- Getting a reputation for trouble
- Getting in over your head
- Getting swell-headed
- Getting too big for your britches
- Getting under people's skin
- Going off half-cocked
- Holding a lit firecracker
- Itching for a fight
- Letting your mouth run ahead of your brain
- Losing your bearings
- Messing with the wrong people
- On a slippery slope

- Opening your big mouth
- Overstepping the mark
- Playing both ends against the middle
- Popping off at everyone
- Putting your foot in it
- Riding rough-shod over everyone
- Rubbing people the wrong way
- Running amok
- Sitting on a powder keg
- Sticking your chin out
- Sticking your neck out
- Stirring the pot
- Testing one's tolerance or patience
- Throwing your chest out
- Throwing your weight around
- Wearing out your welcome

## OR CAN BE DESCRIBED AS:

- Becoming obnoxious
- Being a pain in the ass
- Being a pain in the neck
- Being downright ornery
- Borrowing trouble
- Inviting trouble
- Waving a red flag before the bull

# IN TROUBLE

## GETTING IN TROUBLE IS:

Biting Off More Than He Can Chew, Facing The Wrath Of God, Getting Between A Rock And A Hard Place, Getting Caught With His Pants Down, Getting His Butt In A Sling, Getting His Tail In A Crack, Getting Into Hot Water, Getting More Than He Bargained For, Getting Up To His Neck In Trouble, Getting What He Deserves, Getting What's Coming To Him, Having The Roof Fall In On Him, Painting Himself Into A Corner, Paying The Piper, Pulling Trouble Down Around His Shoulders, Reaping What He Sowed.

## AND CAN BE CHARACTERIZED BY THE FOLLOWING:

- At the end of his rope
- Being hung out to dry
- Being made the scapegoat
- Burned his bridges behind him
- Caught in the switches
- Damned if he does, damned if he doesn't
- Dug his own grave

- Facing the consequences
- Feeling the floor giving way under him
- Feeling the walls closing in on him
- Finding himself standing alone
- Getting cut down to size
- Getting his comeuppance
- Getting his just desserts
- Getting reamed out
- Hanging by a thread
- Hanging on by his fingernails
- Having nowhere to turn
- Having a tough row to hoe
- Having his ears pinned back
- Having his sins coming home to roost
- Having it blow up in his face
- He's in for it
- Hoisted on his own petar

- Hovering between ruin and damnation
- In a peck of trouble
- In a whole mess of trouble
- In dutch
- Left high and dry
- Left holding the bag
- Left in a lurch Left to fend for himself
- Left to his own devices
- Made his bed and has to sleep in it
- No light at the end of the tunnel
- No one to blame but himself
- Paying through the nose
- Running out of excuses
- Staring disaster in the face
- Talked himself into it
- Up against the wall
- Up to his ears in trouble
- Up to his eyeballs in trouble

## OR CAN BE DESCRIBED AS:

- Being in a jam
- Being in a pickle
- Being in a tight squeeze
- Being in deep doo-doo
- Being in dire straits
- Being in the soup

- Being over a barrel
- Being up a tree
- Being up the creek without a paddle
- Getting into the frying pan
- Being backed against the wall

# ESCAPE/AVOID DISASTER

## TO ESCAPE/AVOID DISASTER IS TO:

Beat The Rap, Become Invisible, Break Away, Bust Loose, Buy Your Way Out Of It, Do A Disappearing Act, Escape By A Gnat's Eyelash, Fly The Coop, Get Out By The Skin Of Your Teeth, Get Out In One Piece, Go Free As A Bird, Go Undercover, Hide Out, Head For The Hills, Head For The Woods, Luck Out, Make Yourself Scarce, Melt Into The Crowd, Pull A Houdini, Run For Your Life, Run Like A Scared Rabbit, Save Your Neck, Skip Town, Skirt By, Talk Your Way Out Of It, Weasel Out Of It.

## AND CAN BE CHARACTERIZED BY THE FOLLOWING:

- A narrow escape
- Beating it out of there
- Blasting your way out
- Dropping out of sight
- Getting off scot-free
- Getting out without a scratch
- Getting swallowed up in the city
- Giving them the slip
- Going into hiding
- Going over the wall
- Pulling out in time
- Pulling your coals out of the fire
- Saved by the bell
- Showing them your heels
- Sidestepping it
- Slipping through the noose
- Squeezing through a crack
- Take it on the lam
- Turn tail and run

## OR CAN BE DESCRIBED AS:

- Breaking the chains
- Blowing town
- Bolting out
- Busting loose
- Clearing out
- Crashing out
- Ducking out
- Getting lost
- Going underground
- Jumping ship
- Scooting off
- Slinking away
- Sneaking away
- Squeaking by
- Taking a powder
- Whistling by

# THINGS THAT CAN HAPPEN
# TO YOUR PLANS

## THINGS THAT CAN HAPPEN TO YOUR PLANS ARE:

Fulfillment Of Your Wildest Dreams, Laying On The Shelf, Murphy's Law in Action, Total Fruition.

## AND CAN BE CHARACTERIZED BY THE FOLLOWING:

- Becoming a fantasy
- Being disrupted
- Being interfered with
- Blowing up in your face
- Develop a glitch
- Fading away
- Falling apart
- Falling by the wayside
- Getting sidetracked
- Getting washed out
- Going by the board
- Going up in smoke
- Have a crimp put in them
- Have an end put to them
- Looking ridiculous in hindsight
- Never come to fruition
- Never get off the ground
- They can die

## OR CAN BE DESCRIBED AS:

- Being fulfilled
- Being put on hold
- Going down the tubes
- Withering on the vine

# COMPLETELY DESTROYED

## TO BE COMPLETELY DESTROYED IS TO BE:

Blasted To Pieces, Blown Out Of The Water, Blown Sky High, Blown To Eternity, Blown To Hell, Blown To Kingdom Come, Blown To Smithereens, Bombed To Bits, Demolished, Leveled To The Ground, Nuked, Ripped To Shreds, Scattered To The Four Winds, Sent Up In Smoke, Strewn From Pillar To Post, Torn Asunder, Wasted, Wiped Off The Face Of The Earth, Wiped Out.

## AND CAN BE CHARACTERIZED BY THE FOLLOWING:

- Being spread all over the lot
- Destroyed beyond recognition
- Nothing left but a memory

## OR CAN BE DESCRIBED AS:

- Being reduced to ashes
- Being reduced to rubble
- Being utterly destroyed

# DIMINISH AN INFLATED EGO

## TO DIMINISH AN INFLATED EGO IS TO:

Burst One's Balloon, Burst One's Bubble, Knock The Stilts Out From Under Someone, Let The Air Out Of Someone's Tires, Pull The Rug Out From Under Someone, Puncture The Windbag, Stick A Pin In Someone's Balloon, Strip Away His Facade, Take Someone Down A Peg Or Two.

## AND CAN BE CHARACTERIZED BY THE FOLLOWING:

- Beating him at his own game
- Bringing his faults out in the open
- Calling his bluff
- Exposing the idol's clay feet
- Facing up to him
- Finding his Achille's heel
- Finding the kinks in his armor
- Giving him a dose of his own medicine
- Giving him his comeuppance
- Knocking him off his high horse
- Knocking him off his pedestal
- Making him put his money where his mouth is
- Making one look foolish
- Revealing one as a paper tiger
- Showing him up for what he is
- Taking the starch out of him
- Turning the tables on him

## OR CAN BE DESCRIBED AS:

- Taking the wind out of someone's sails

# ASTOUND SOMEONE

## TO ASTOUND SOMEONE IS TO:

Flabbergast Him, Knock Him For A Loop, Knock The Stilts Out From Under Him, Leave Him Numb, Make Him Gasp, Make His Eyes Pop, Make His Head Spin, Make His Jaw Drop, Rock Him, Send Him Spinning, Set Him Back On His Heels, Shake Him Up, Shock The Wits Out Of Him, Stagger His Imagination, Stand Him On His Ear, Stop Him Dead In His Tracks, Stupefy Him, Stun Him, Zap Him, Zonk Him.

## AND CAN BE CHARACTERIZED BY THE FOLLOWING:

- Blowing his mind
- Cutting him off at the knees
- Driving him bananas
- Driving him bonkers
- Driving him crazy
- Driving him out of his mind
- Knocking the wind out of him
- Pulling the rug out from under him
- Racking him up
- Sending him reeling

## OR CAN BE DESCRIBED AS:

- Leaving someone dumbfounded
- Leaving someone speechless

# CHALLENGE/COMPETE

## TO CHALLENGE/COMPETE IS TO:

Back One In A Corner, Back One To The Wall, Badger Someone, Bug Someone, Butt Heads, Call Someone Out, Call Someone's Bluff, Carry The Fight To Someone, Come To Blows With Someone, Corner Someone, Draw A Line In The Sand, Face Up To Someone, Get In A Push-And-Shove Match, Get In A Rhubarb With Someone, Get On Someone's Back, Get Physical With Someone,

Go A Couple Of Rounds With One, Have A Showdown, Have Fisticuffs, Lock Horns With Someone, Meet Someone Head-On, Push Someone Around, Put On The Gloves With One, Put Someone To The Test, Put Up Your Dukes, Put Your Fists Up To Someone, Spar With Someone, Stand Up To Someone, Step In The Ring With One, Take The Bull By The Horns, Tell Someone Off.

## AND CAN BE CHARACTERIZED BY THE FOLLOWING:

- Asking one what he's going to do
- Becoming aggressive
- Being a constant source of trouble
- Being a thorn in one's side
- Getting downright nasty about it
- Getting someone's back up
- Getting someone's dander up
- Giving an eye for an eye, a tooth for a tooth
- Being prepared to draw
- Bringing matters to a head
- Coming on strong
- Giving one a slap in the face
- Giving someone a hard time
- Giving someone an ultimatum
- Giving tit for tat
- Having a belligerent attitude
- Irritating the life out of someone
- Leaving no room for compromise
- Leaving someone no choice
- Making it a matter of pride
- Meeting one eye-to-eye
- Meeting someone on his turf

- Out for blood
- Putting someone in an untenable position
- Putting someone on the spot
- Putting the heat on someone
- Putting the pressure on one
- Putting your honor on the line
- Putting your reputation on the line
- Refusing to back down
- Refusing to budge
- Refusing to give an inch
- Refusing to take someone's guff
- Rubbing someone's nose in it
- Settling things for once and for all
- Spoiling for trouble
- Sticking out your chin
- Taking a challenge
- Taking a dare
- Telling one to choose his weapon
- Telling one to put up or shut up
- Throwing down the gauntlet
- Throwing your weight around
- Tweaking someone's nose
- Winner takes all

## OR CAN BE DESCRIBED AS:

- Banging heads with someone
- Going head-to-head with someone
- Going to the mat with someone

- Squaring off with someone
- Standing toe-to-toe with someone
- Taking someone on

# NOT AS PLANNED / UNEXPECTED

## WHEN THINGS ARE NOT GOING SO WELL, IT IS A:

Bad-Hair Day, Catch-22 Situation, Disaster, Fine Kettle Of Fish, Jinx, No-Win Situation, Revolting Development, Sad State Of Affairs, Weird Turn Of Events.

## AND CAN BE CHARACTERIZED BY THE FOLLOWING:

- A victim of the fickle finger of fate
- And the worst is yet to come!
- Beat before he stepped in the ring
- Can't get a handle on it
- Can't put the brakes on it
- Can't win for losing
- Damned if I do, damned if I don't
- Doom and gloom
- Everything I touch turns to ashes
- Feeling the world closing in on me
- Finding problems at every turn
- Getting off to a bad start
- Getting up on the wrong side of the bed

- If it isn't one thing, it's another
- If it wasn't for bad luck, he wouldn't have any luck at all
- It just hit the fan
- It never rains but it pours
- Like a ship without a rudder
- Not my day!
- On the skids
- One thing leads to another
- Problems coming out of the woodwork
- Should have stayed in bed
- The ground is giving way under my feet
- The roof is falling in on me
- Troubles growing like topsy
- Watching my dreams going up in smoke
- What a mess!

## OR CAN BE DESCRIBED AS:

- Bottoming out
- Going downhill rapidly
- Going from bad to worse
- Hitting bottom

# BADLY DEFEATED

## TO BE BADLY DEFEATED IS TO BE:

Battered And Bruised, Beaten Into The Ground, Beaten To A Fare-Thee- Well, Beaten To A Pulp, Carried Out On A Stretcher, Knocked From Pillar To Post, Knocked Senseless, Laid Out Like A Rug, Stomped Flatter Than A Pancake, Taken Apart Limb By Limb.

## AND CAN BE CHARACTERIZED BY THE FOLLOWING:

- Battered beyond recognition
- Beaten within an inch of your life
- Having the stuffing kicked out of you
- Knocking out every tooth in his head
- Left for dead
- Having your brains beat out
- Having your head handed to you
- Knocking his lights out
- Taking the licking of your life

## OR CAN BE DESCRIBED AS:

- Being whipped

# REVENGE IS SWEET

## SWEET REVENGE IS:

Bad-Mouthing Someone, Baiting A Trap For Someone, Blackballing One, Burning Someone In Effigy, Digging A Hole For One To Fall Into, Digging

Up Dirt On One, Dragging Someone's Name Through The Mud, Giving One
A Dose Of His Own Medicine, Greasing The Skids For One, Lighting The
Fuse On One, Plotting One's Downfall, Putting A Hex On Someone, Putting
The Shoe On The Other Foot, Setting Someone Up, Sharpening The Knife For
One, Slipping The Noose Around One's Neck, Spreading Stories About Some-
one, Sticking Pins In A Doll For Someone, Throwing Darts At One's Picture,
Undermining Someone, Waging A Vendetta Against One.

## AND CAN BE CHARACTERIZED BY THE FOLLOWING:

- An eye for an eye, a tooth for a tooth
- Biding your time to get even
- Building a case against someone
- Carrying a grudge
- Giving him enough rope to hang himself
- Giving him the evil eye
- Going behind one's back
- Going to hoist him on his own petard
- Having a bone to pick with someone
- Having a bullet with his name on it
- Having a score to settle with someone
- Having a thing stuck in your craw
- Having it in for someone
- Having one in your sights
- Having one on your hit list
- Having one's grave marked
- Having someone marked
- Having the knife out for someone
- He's a marked man!
- His name is mud!
- Holding it in for someone
- Itching to pay someone back
- Laying a trap for someone
- Let's see how he likes it!
- Lurking in the bushes for someone
- Lying in wait for someone
- Needing to get something off your chest
- Now it's my turn at bat!
- One of these days!
- Out to get someone
- Out to settle his hash
- Out to submarine someone
- Planning one's demise
- Planning to rub his nose in it
- Ready to pounce on him
- Waiting for one to make a wrong move
- Waiting for someone to slip up
- Waiting for the right time
- Waiting in the bushes for one
- Waiting to get back at one
- Waiting to get even
- What's good for the goose is good for the gander!
- Will pay him back in spades
- Will repay him with interest
- Writing one's epitaph

# UNFRIENDLY RELATIONS

## UNFRIENDLY RELATIONS ARE:

Bitter Enemies, Clashing Personalities, Downhill Relations, Like Flint And Steel, Mismatched Pairs, Mortal Enemies.

## OR CAN BE DESCRIBED AS:

- Evening the score
- Paying someone back in kind—tit for tat!

## AND CAN BE CHARACTERIZED BY THE FOLLOWING:

- As different as night and day
- At a stalemate
- At different ends of the pole
- At each other's throat
- At loggerheads
- At odds with each other
- At sixes and sevens
- Avoiding each other like the plague
- Bad blood between them
- Bumping heads with each other
- Can't agree on the time of day
- Can't be civil to each other
- Can't get along
- Can't stand the sight of one
- Can't stand to be in the same room with each other
- Constantly having words
- Crossing swords with each other
- Detesting each other
- Don't have a thing in common
- Don't speak to each other
- Getting nowhere fast
- Going their separate ways
- Growing further apart
- Hate each others' guts
- He disgusts me!
- He grates on my nerves!
- He turns my stomach!
- I won't have anything to do with him!
- I wouldn't date him if he were the last man on earth!
- I wouldn't give her the time of day!
- I wouldn't give him the sweat off my brow!
- I wouldn't lift a finger to help him!
- If he were drowning, I'd throw him an anchor!
- If I never see her again, it will be too soon!
- If she says "white", he'll say "black"

- Irritate each other
- It's a Mexican stand-off
- Mix like oil and water
- Never mentions his name
- No love lost between them
- Not in harmony
- On different wave lengths
- On opposite sides of a question
- On the outs
- Out of sync with each other
- Out of touch with their feelings
- Rubbing each other the wrong way
- Screaming at each other
- She leaves him cold
- She makes me sick!
- She turns me off!
- Stepping on each other's toes
- There's no good in him to give!
- They look for ways to disagree
- This town is too small for both of us!
- Throwing up at the mention of one's name
- Totally different people
- When they meet, sparks fly
- When they meet, the fur flies
- Worlds apart on everything

## OR CAN BE DESCRIBED AS:

- Bandying words
- Fighting like cats and dogs
- Shunning each other

# MAKE A MISTAKE

## TO MAKE A MISTAKE IS TO:

Blow It, Boot The Ball, Choke, Commit A Blunder, Flub It, Foul Up, Get Egg On Your Face, Goof Up, Make A Bum Decision, Make A Glitch, Screw Up, Stumble.

## AND CAN BE CHARACTERIZED BY THE FOLLOWING:

- Dropping the ball
- Failing to see what was staring you in the face
- Falling flat on your face
- Fouling it up beyond all recognition
- Going astray
- Having an act boomerang

- Letting something get away from you
- Letting something slip through your fingers
- Missing the boat

- Overlooking the obvious
- Putting your foot in it
- Putting your foot in the bucket
- Tripping over your own feet

## OR CAN BE DESCRIBED AS:

- Making a boo-boo
- Messing up
- Tripping up

# HEADING FOR TROUBLE

## HEADING FOR TROUBLE IS:

Beginning To Wink At Your Sins, Getting Careless, Getting Cocky, Getting Out Of Hand, Getting Over Confident, Getting Too Close To The Fire, Getting Too Smart For Your Own Good, Hanging Out With Bad Company, Ignoring The Warning Signs, Making A Mockery Of The Rules, Not Doing Your Homework, Not Minding The Store, Not Watching Your P's And Q's, Not Watching Your Step, Overstepping The Mark, Playing Fast And Loose, Riding For A Fall, Skirting Danger, Straying From The Fold, Taking Short Cuts, Taking The Path Of Least Resistance, Taking Too Much For Granted, Walking Too Close To The Edge.

## AND CAN BE CHARACTERIZED BY THE FOLLOWING:

- Acting like a know-it-all
- Beginning to believe your own resume
- Beginning to fray around the edges
- Beginning to lose your grip
- Challenging the odds
- Cruising for a bruising

- Cutting it too close
- Doesn't see the handwriting on the wall
- Drifting without a rudder
- Getting in over your head
- Getting in the deep woods
- Getting off base

- Getting sloppy in your dealings
- Getting soft in the head
- Getting too puffed up with yourself
- Going downhill fast
- Having a tiger by the tail
- Heeding the siren's call
- Kicking over the traces
- Leaving yourself wide open
- Letting success go to your head
- Letting your pride dull your senses
- Letting yourself get rusty
- Losing contact with yourself
- Losing your compass
- Losing your edge
- Losing your sense of direction
- Letting your guard down
- Moving in the wrong circles
- On the skids
- Overplaying your hand
- Resting on your laurels
- Resting on your oars
- Setting yourself up as a target
- Shooting from the hip
- Starting to need a larger hat size
- Taking long shots
- Taking on more than you can handle
- Taking your eye off the ball
- Too sure of yourself
- Trying to run the whole show
- Walking on eggs

## OR CAN BE DESCRIBED AS:

- Getting in deep water
- Going down the wrong path
- Going off the deep end
- Skating on thin ice
- Straying far afield
- Treading in deep water

# RUNNING AFOUL OF THE LAW

## TO BECOME INVOLVED WITH THE LAW IS TO:

Blow The Whistle On Someone, Get A Rap, Get Busted, Get Collared, Get Dragged Before The Judge, Get Hauled Into Court, Get Nabbed, Get Picked Up, Get Pinched, Get Sent To The Clinker, Get Sent To The Hoosegow, Get The Book Thrown At You, Get Thrown In The Slammer, Get Ticketed, Get Worked Over, Get Your Rap Sheet Pulled, Go To Jail, Go To The Big House, Go To The Pen, Put The Finger On Someone, Run Afoul Of The Law, Turn Someone In.

## AND CAN BE CHARACTERIZED BY THE FOLLOWING:

- A dirk
- A gat
- A piece
- A record as long as your arm
- A repeater; three-time loser
- A shiv
- An equalizer
- Beating the rap
- Breaking every law in the book
- Canary
- Caught with the smoking gun
- Clean as a whistle
- Coming down hard on you
- Con
- Copping a plea
- Copping out
- Dead wrong
- Doing hard time
- Doing time
- Facing a hanging judge
- Fessing up
- Fink
- First-time offender
- Fixing a jury
- Getting a bum rap
- Getting a slap on the wrist
- Getting bailed out
- Getting caught with the goods
- Getting caught with your hand in the cookie jar
- Getting off easy
- Getting sprung
- Getting the third degree
- Getting two lashes with a wet noodle
- Going scot free
- Having your rights read to you
- He flew the coop
- Hiring a mouthpiece
- Holing up
- Informer
- Inmate
- Jailbird
- Jumping bail
- Knocking over a place
- Lifer
- Locked you up and threw away the key
- Lowered the boom on you
- Nailed dead to rights
- Nailed to the wall
- On bread and water
- On the bad side of the law
- On the lam
- On the run
- Plea bargaining
- Pulling a heist
- Rat
- Reading you chapter and verse
- Receiving a stiff sentence
- Scofflaw
- Screw
- Singing like a canary
- Spilling your guts
- Stool pigeon
- Stoolie
- Sweating it out
- Taking the fifth
- Walking the streets
- Went over the wall
- Yardbird

## OR CAN BE DESCRIBED AS:

- Being put in bracelets
- Getting nailed
- Making the wanted list
- The fix is in
- Three strikes are out
- Turn state's evidence
- Walk

# RECKLESS

## TO BE RECKLESS IS TO:

Dare The Devil, Do Things Helter-Skelter, Fly In The Face Of Danger, Go Off Half-Cocked, Have A Devil-May-Care Attitude, Have More Guts Than Sense, Ignore The Warning Signs, Play Fast And Loose, Rush Into Things, Shoot First And Ask Questions Later, Taunt Fate, Wave A Red Flag Before The Bull.

## AND CAN BE CHARACTERIZED BY THE FOLLOWING:

- A bull in a china shop
- An accident waiting to happen
- Blurting things out
- Letting the chips fall where they may
- Putting your foot in your mouth
- Your mouth is faster than your brain
- Shooting from the hip
- Shooting off your mouth
- Sticking your neck out
- Talking your way into trouble
- Throwing caution to the wind

## OR CAN BE DESCRIBED AS:

- Being addle-headed
- Being hotheaded
- Laughing at danger
- Running amok

# TO PERSEVERE

## TO PERSEVERE IS TO:

Barrel In, Bounce Back, Come Back Like A Shot, Come Back Swinging, Come Back With A Vengeance, Come Blazing Back, Come Off The Floor, Face The Lion In His Den, Get Back In The Saddle, Get Your Irish Up, Go For The Jugular, Pick Yourself Up And Come Back For More, Pour It On, Return To The Fray, Ride The Bronc, Storm Back, Take A Deep Breath And Wade In.

## AND CAN BE CHARACTERIZED BY THE FOLLOWING:

- A hero dies once, a coward dies a thousand times
- Becoming more determined
- Being undeterred
- Bringing renewed energy
- Brushing off the setback
- Calling up your reserves
- Coming alive
- Digging your heels in
- Fighting like a tiger
- Finding new courage
- Getting back on the horse that threw you
- Getting revitalized
- Getting your adrenelin pumping
- Getting your back up
- Getting your second wind
- Giving as good as you take
- Giving it all you've got
- Going at it as if your life depended on it
- Going for broke
- Gritting your teeth
- Hanging in there
- Hanging on like a pit bull
- Picking up the pace
- Planting your feet
- Refusing to quit
- Setting your jaw
- Shaking it off and plowing in
- Showing one what you're made of
- Starting to get serious
- Sticking it out
- Swinging into action
- Turning up the heat
- Wearing your scars like a badge of honor

## OR CAN BE DESCRIBED AS:

- Making a comeback

# PAYING THE PRICE FOR WRONGDOING

## WHEN YOU PAY THE PRICE FOR WRONGDOING, YOU:

Get Drummed Out Of Polite Society, Get Taken Down A Peg, Get Taught A Lesson, Get Treated Like A Leper, Get What You Deserve, Get What's Coming To You, Get Your Comeuppance, Get Your Just Desserts, Have Dogs Set Upon You, Have Fingers Pointed At You, Have People Coming After You With A Rope, Have People Laughing Behind Your Back, Have Rotten Eggs Thrown At You, Have To Pay The Fiddler, Have Your Balloon Punctured, Have Your Last Shred Of Self-Respect Taken Away From You, Have Your Sins Come Home To Roost, Lie In The Bed You Made For Yourself, Pay The Piper, Pay Through The Nose, Reap What You Sow, Rue The Day You Were Bom, Suffer Ignominy And Defeat, Wish You Knew Then What You Know Now.

## AND CAN BE CHARACTERIZED BY THE FOLLOWING:

- Being left crying in your beer
- Being left high and dry to fend for yourself
- Ending up alone, out in the cold
- Ending up in the gutter
- Feeling like you're on a desert island
- Finding doors closed against you
- Finding no one will have anything to do with you
- Finding people avoiding you
- Finding what goes around comes around
- Getting shown up for what you are
- Having children shy away from you
- Having egg on your face
- Having it thrown up in your face
- Having no one to turn to
- Having only yourself to blame
- Having people avoid you
- Having people turn away from you in disgust
- Having the bottom drop out of your life
- Having the floor give way under you
- Having the world crash down around your ears
- Having your bubble burst
- Having your shortcomings bared
- Having your sins come back to haunt you

- Learning the hard way
- Losing face

- Not having a friend left in the world

## OR CAN BE DESCRIBED AS:

- Becoming a pariah
- Becoming a personna non grata
- Becoming the talk of the town
- Being dumped
- Being held up as a sad example
- Being held up to public ridicule
- Being ignored
- Being left to lick your wounds

- Being made a laughingstock
- Being made the butt of jokes
- Being pilloried
- Being put in the stock
- Being put on public display
- Being ridden out of town on a rail
- Being spat upon Being tarred and feathered

# XVII
# THE WORLD OF WORK

# OCCUPATIONS

## OCCUPATIONS ARE:

Careers, Day Jobs, Professions, Trades, Vocations.

## AND CAN BE CHARACTERIZED BY THE FOLLOWING:

- Actor
- Actress
- Administrator
- Athlete
- Auto mechanic
- Aviatrix
- Boxer
- Carpenter
- Chiropractor
- Clergyman
- Cook
- Doctor
- Doorman
- Electrician
- Farmer
- Garbage collector
- Government worker
- Laborer
- Lawyer
- Mechanic
- Money-lender
- Nurse
- Office worker
- Ophthalmologist
- Painter
- Pilot
- Plumber
- Policeman
- Policewoman
- Politician
- Practicing physician
- Private investigator
- Psychiatrist
- Psychologist
- Salesman
- Secretary
- Specialist
- Surgeon
- Teacher
- TV Talk-show host
- Urologist
- Weatherman
- Wrestler

## OR CAN BE DESCRIBED AS:

- Ambulance chaser
- Angel of mercy
- Babysitter
- Barracuda
- Bloodsucker
- Blue-coat
- Bone-crusher
- Butcher

- Contortionist
- Cop
- Copper
- Crook
- Desk-jockey
- Drip doctor
- Eye doctor
- Feeder-at-the-trough
- Fender-bender
- Flusher-pusher
- Fuzz
- Fly-boy
- Fly-girl
- Girl Friday
- Grease-monkey
- Grunt-and-groaner
- Guesser
- Gumshoe
- Hack
- Ham
- Hash-slinger
- Hayseed
- Head-shrinker
- Holy Joe Jocks
- Legal beagle
- Loan-shark
- Mouthpiece
- Nail-banger
- Padre
- Panhandler
- Paper-shuffler
- Peddler
- Pee-pusher
- Pencil-pusher
- Pick-and-shoveler
- Pig
- Pill-pusher
- Plow-jockey
- Politico
- Preacher
- Private eye
- Psychobabbler
- Pug
- Quack
- Sanitary engineer
- Sawbones
- Shocker
- Shrink
- Shylock
- Sleuth
- Spatterer
- Steno
- Talking-head
- Tax-burden
- Tech Tinkerer
- Trash disposer
- Wall artist
- Ward-heeler
- Whistle-blower Wire-man

# THE POWERS THAT BE

## THE POWERS THAT BE ARE:

Big-Shots, Big-Wigs, Bosses, Decision-Makers, Head-Honchos, Big Chiefs, The Front Office, The Ones In Authority, The Ones In Charge, The Ones Who Set The Rules, The Order-Givers, The People Upstairs, The Rein Holders, The Whip-Crackers, They Who Foot The Bills, They Who Write The Script.

## AND CAN BE CHARACTERIZED BY THE FOLLOWING:

- At the helm
- At the top
- Call the shots
- Drive the herd
- Give the okay
- Has the whip-hand
- Have the say-so
- In the driver's seat
- In whose lap it is in
- It is up to him
- Make the calls
- Number one
- On the top rung of the ladder
- Point the way
- Runs the show
- Solely responsible
- Steers the boat
- Where the buck stops

## OR CAN BE DESCRIBED AS:

- Captain of the ship
- Commander
- Czar
- Dictator
- Director of the scene
- Leader of the pack
- Lord and master
- Ruler of the roost
- The coach
- Those in the ivory tower
- Those who lay down the law

# EMPLOYEES

**EMPLOYEES ARE:**

Bakers, Blue-Collars, Buck-Passers, Butchers, Craft Persons, Girls-Friday, Grunts, Hired Hands, Indians, Old Hands, Old-Timers, Part-Timers, Pencil-Pushers, Peons, Pick-And-Shovelers, Rank-And-Filers, Stable Hands, Stage Hands, Straw Bosses, The Cogs In The Wheel, The Crews, The Help, The Minions, The Troops, The Water-Cooler Gang.

**AND CAN BE CHARACTERIZED BY THE FOLLOWING:**

- Behind the scenes
- Chained to the desk
- Not paid to think
- Paid to take orders
- Punch the clock
- Shuffle papers
- Voices on telephones

**OR CAN BE DESCRIBED AS:**

- Aides
- Assistants
- Clock watchers
- Coolies
- Floor-walkers
- Garden varieties
- Road gangs
- Serfs
- Staffs
- Subordinates
- The run-of-the-mine
- Wage slaves
- Workers

# INEXPERIENCED WORKER

**AN INEXPERIENCED WORKER IS A:**

Fresh Kid, Greenhorn, Half-Baked Apprentice, Kid In Short Pants, New Kid On The Block, Raw Recruit, Rookie, Snivel-Nosed Freshman, Tenderfoot, Tyro, Wide-Eyed Beginner, Wide-Eyed Innocent, Young Pup, Young Turk.

## AND CAN BE CHARACTERIZED BY THE FOLLOWING:

- Cutting his baby teeth on it
- Didn't do his homework
- Doesn't have it all together
- Doesn't know which end is up
- Goes off half-cocked
- Has big shoes to fill
- Hasn't got his feet on the ground
- Hasn't had a baptism by fire
- Hasn't learned the ropes
- Hasn't learned the score
- Hasn't shaved yet
- Ill-prepared
- In over his head
- Is raw material
- Just getting his feet wet
- Just out of diapers
- Learning his way around
- Needs breaking in
- Out of his league
- Smart aleck
- Stumbling over his own feet
- Unsure of his footing

## OR CAN BE DESCRIBED AS:

- A boy sent to do a man's job
- A lamb among wolves
- An uninitiated amateur
- An upstart
- Freshman on the job
- Fuzz-faced
- Green as grass
- Still tied to his mother's apron strings
- Still wet behind the ears
- Unschooled and untutored

# SEASONED WORKER

## A SEASONED WORKER IS A:

Crusty Old Character, Diehard, Grey-Beard Retread, Grizzly Old Bear, Old Codger, Old Coot, Old Goat, Old Grey Mare, Old Timer, Patriarch, Stodgy Old Character, Veteran, Wizened Old Man.

## AND CAN BE CHARACTERIZED BY THE FOLLOWING:

- Been around the block a few times
- Can do it with his eyes closed
- Can't teach an old dog new tricks

- Forgot more about it than you'll ever learn
- Knows every trick in the book
- Knows his way around
- Knows it backwards and forwards
- Knows it like the back of his hand

- Learned the hard way
- Lives in the good old days
- Paid his dues Set in his ways
- Stuck in the rut
- Throwback to the old days
- Wrote the book on it

## OR CAN BE DESCRIBED AS:

- An old hand at the job
- An old salt

# PRIOR EXPERIENCE

## PRIOR EXPERIENCE IS WHEN YOU'VE:

Been Burned, Been Singed, Been There, Been To The School Of Hard Knocks, Gotten Wised Up, Had It Burned Into Your Brain, Learned A Lesson You'll Never Forget, Learned From Doing, Learned The Hard Way, Learned Your Lesson, Paid Your Dues, Received A Liberal Education.

## AND CAN BE CHARACTERIZED BY THE FOLLOWING:

- Burnt child dreads the fire
- Can't teach an old dog new tricks
- Chalked it up to experience
- Digging up the past
- Dragging it by again!
- Everything changes, but everything stays the same
- Getting a second bite of the apple

- Getting too soon old, too late smart
- Hardened and refined in the crucible of life
- Having a memory like an elephant
- Having bad memories of it
- Having the scars to prove it
- History repeats itself
- How could I forget!

- I read that book!
- I remember it like it was yesterday
- I remember it well!
- I'd just as soon forget it!
- If I had my life to live over!
- If I knew then what I know now
- It takes one to know one
- It's fresh in my mind
- It's old hat
- I've got a long memory!
- Just more of the same
- Like a voice out of the past
- Man fools you once, shame on him; Two times, shame on you! Never again!
- No fool like an old fool
- Now I know better
- Older and wiser
- Once is enough!
- Opening old sores
- Rehash of old baloney
- Ressurecting bad memories
- Same old dish warmed over
- Same old scam with a fresh coat of paint
- Same old song and dance
- Some people never learn!
- The good old days!
- The song lingers on
- There's snow on the roof, but there's fire in the basement
- They are reinventing the wheel
- They don't make them like they used to
- What goes around comes around
- When I was young and foolish
- When men were men and women appreciated it
- Won't bite a second time!
- Won't make the same mistake twice
- Wouldn't touch it with a ten-foot pole!

**OR CAN BE DESCRIBED AS:**

- Having been down this road before
- Having heard that song before
- Having learned it at your mother's knee

# AGREE WITH A PROPOSAL

**TO AGREE WITH A PROPOSAL IS TO:**

Applaud The Decision, Back It Up, Beat The Drum For It, Boost It, Cheer It On, Express Your Support, Extol Its Virtues, Give It Kudos, Get On The

Bandwagon, Give It Your Stamp Of Approval, Praise It to High Heaven, Praise It To The Sky, Register Your Approval, Sing Its Praises, Throw In With The Suggestion.

## AND CAN BE CHARACTERIZED BY THE FOLLOWING:

- Accepting it lock, stock and barrel
- Agreeing with it wholeheartedly
- Bragging about it
- Finding it appealing
- Getting behind the move
- Joining the effort
- Joining the parade
- Latching onto the idea
- Lauding the accomplishment
- Lending your support
- Pitching in to help
- Talking it up
- Thinking it's the greatest thing that
- came down the pike
- Touting its merits to the world

## OR CAN BE DESCRIBED AS:

- Being nuts about it
- Being wild about it
- Endorsing the idea
- Giving it your okay
- Going bananas over it

# DISAGREE WITH A PROPOSAL

## TO DISAGREE WITH A PROPOSAL IS TO:

Approach It From Another Angle, Find Fault With Every Detail, Kick Up A Fuss, Rip It Asunder, Say It's The Pits, Shoot It Full Of Holes, Take Exception To It, Take Violent Exception To It, Tear It To Shreds, Tear The Idea Apart, Tell The Other Side Of The Story.

## AND CAN BE CHARACTERIZED BY THE FOLLOWING:

- Belittling their opinions
- Busting their chops
- Challenging their judgment
- Creating unrest
- Disagreeing with it every step of the way

- Disrupting the proceedings
- Finding it runs against your grain
- Finding it revolting
- Giving them a piece of your mind
- Giving them an earful
- Nailing them to the wall
- Rocking the boat
- Screaming to high heaven
- Seeing things another way

- Shattering their illusions
- Showing them the error of their ways
- Stirring up trouble
- Taking an opposite approach
- Taking on the establishment
- Taking their argument apart
- Taking issue with them
- Taking them to task
- Telling them where they can go
- Telling them where to get off

## OR CAN BE DESCRIBED AS:

- Beating their ears
- Blasting them
- Burning their ears

- Giving them both barrels
- Unloading on them

# DELAY ACTION ON A PROPOSAL

## TO DELAY ACTION ON A PROPOSAL IS TO:

Chew On It, Dawdle Over It, Dilly-Dally Over It, Dissect It, Do Flip- Flops On It, Drag Your Feet On It, Fiddle With It, Fiddle-Faddle Around It, File It Away For Later, Ham-String It, Hem And Haw Over It, Hesitate About It, Hold It In Abeyance, Lay It Aside, Leave It In Limbo, Leave It Twisting In The Wind, Leave It Up In The Air, Let It Gather Dust, Let It Linger, Let It Ride, Let It Simmer, Let It Wait, Mark Time On It, Nit-Pick It, Pass Over It, Ponder It, Postpone It, Pussyfoot Around With It, Put It In Your Back Pocket, Put It On Hold, Put It On The Back Burner, Put It Under A Microscope, Quibble About It, Send It Back To Square One, Shelve It, Shuffle It Around, Sit On It, Straddle The Issue, Study It To Death, Table It.

## AND CAN BE CHARACTERIZED BY THE FOLLOWING:

- Bickering on it Booting it around

- Changeable as the weather

- Crossing every "t", dotting every "I"
- Depends on whose ox is being gored
- Doing first things first
- Drive it or park it!
- Fish or cut bait!
- Giving it a low priority
- Giving it scant attention
- Going over it with a fine-toothed comb
- Having mixed feelings about it
- Having one foot on either side of the question
- Having no mind of his own
- Having second thoughts about it
- Ignore it and hope it will go away
- Kicking it back and forth
- Kicking it from pillar to post
- Letting it hang fire
- Maybe yes, maybe no
- Mulling it over
- Sending it back to the drawing board
- Sending it to a committee
- Sitting on the fence
- Stewing over it
- Studying every detail
- Swallow it or spit it out!
- Swaying with the wind
- Takes forever for him to make up his mind
- Taking it under advisement
- Taking your own sweet time
- Thinking about it later
- Tossing a coin
- Won't take a stand on it

## OR CAN BE DESCRIBED AS:

- Being a Scarlett O'Hara—think about it tomorrow
- Being fickle about it
- Being wishy-washy about it
- Dragging it out
- Placing it in the bottom of the stack
- Putting it back in the in-file
- Putting it off for tomorrow
- Putting it off until the last minute
- Putting it on the bottom of the list
- Waffling on it

# TO DISMISS SOMEONE

## TO DISMISS SOMEONE IS TO:

Boot Him Out, Can Him, Cancel Him, Cashier Him, Drop Him Like A Hot Potato, Dump Him, Feed Him To The Sharks, Give Him The Axe, Give Him

The Boot, Give Him The Bum's Rush, Give One The Heave- Ho, Give One The Pink Slip, Pull The Plug On Someone, Put Him At Liberty, Put The Skids To Him, Sack Him, Send Him On His Way, Send Him Packing, Show Him The Door, Terminate Someone, Throw Him Out, Throw Him Out On His Ear, Throw Him To The Wolves, Turn Him Out In The Cold, Turn Him Out To Pasture, Unload Him, Write Him Off.

## AND CAN BE CHARACTERIZED BY THE FOLLOWING:

- Blowing him out
- Dropping him from the payroll
- Kicking him upstairs
- Locking him out
- Putting him out on the street
- Putting him in the unemployment line
- Shipping him to Siberia
- Taking away his living
- Taking away his bread and butter

## OR CAN BE DESCRIBED AS:

- Firing someone
- Getting rid of someone
- Giving him his walking papers

# About the Author

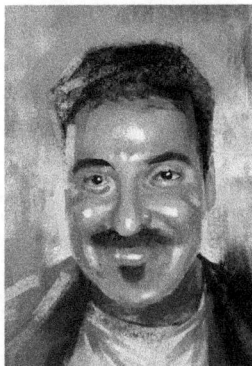

J. Ajlouny was born in Detroit in 1958, the only son of immigrants from Ramallah, Palestine. His father was a member of the US Army who served in Japan and South Korea during the Korean War. After raising six children, his mother became a public-school ESL educator. Both were active members of their church and community organizations.

Mr. Ajlouny graduated from Wayne State University in Detroit in 1979 with a B.A. in Journalism. A London, England, based art gallery and print publisher hired him as a writer and promoter of fine art, including original limited-edition prints, rare books, and manuscripts. He attended night classes at Detroit College of Law (now Michigan State University College of Law) and earned a J.D. in 1983, but never fully engaged in the practice of law, preferring to make a career in art and literature instead. A series of opportunities took him from the newspaper syndication business to book publishing and a thriving literary and talent agency. In 1998 he incorporated these various concerns into an umbrella organization called the Federal Bureau of Entertainment. The principal focus of FBE was the development, production, and staging of one-person stage shows featuring notable British actors whose performances highlighted important literary texts from Shakespeare to Orwell.

Now in ungainly but blissful retirement, J. Ajlouny has resumed his writing career and is devoting himself to touring theatre projects and topical research in Great Lakes history. He is a Reader in History at the Library of Congress and the William Clements Library at the University of Michigan.

# Topical Index

# The Fresh Ink Group

Publishing
Free Memberships
Share & Read Free Stories, Essays, Articles
Free-Story Newsletter
Writing Contests

&

Books
E-books
Amazon Bookstore

&

Authors
Editors
Artists
Professionals
Publishing Services
Publisher Resources

&

Members' Websites
Members' Blogs
Social Media

FreshInkGroup.com
**Email: info@FreshInkGroup.com**
**Twitter: @FreshInkGroup**
**Google+: Fresh Ink Group**
**Facebook.com/FreshInkGroup**
**LinkedIn: Fresh Ink Group**
**About.me/FreshInkGroup**

**Fresh Ink** Group
Guntersville

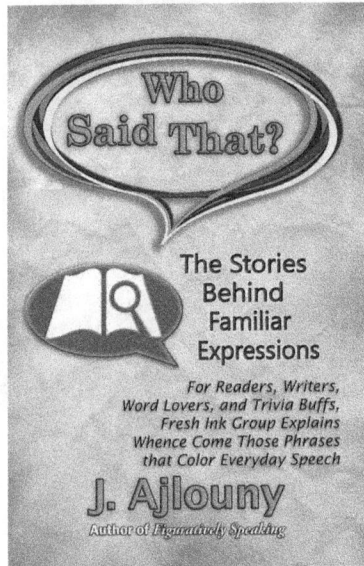

**Who Said That?**

The Stories Behind Familiar Expressions

By J. Ajlouny

*Who Said That?* provides an entertaining and authoritative reference for the origins and meanings of our common figures of speech.

- Who said 100+ famous expressions?
- Who *really* said them?
- What did they actually say?
- What did they actually mean?
- Why did they say them that way?
- Who repeated what was said?

Surprisingly true, sometimes strange, always fascinating, the stories about whence came these expressions will entertain, educate, and even amaze you.

**FreshInkGroup.com**

www.ingramcontent.com/pod-product-compliance
Lightning Source LLC
Chambersburg PA
CBHW050112280326
41933CB00010B/1064